The Masters of
SHOW JUMPING

The Masters of SHOW JUMPING

Ann Martin

HOWELL BOOK HOUSE
NEW YORK
1991

A SALAMANDER BOOK

Copyright © 1991 by Salamander Books Ltd.

Howell Book House
Macmillan Publishing Company
866 Third Avenue, New York, NY 10022

Library of Congress Cataloging-in-Publication Data

Martin, Ann
    Masters of show jumping/Ann Martin
        p.   cm.
    ISBN 0-87605-893-4
    1. Show jumpers (Persons)—Great Britain—
    Biography.   I. Title.
SF295.53.M37   1991
798.2′5′0922—dc20   90 - 15527
                                       CIP

CREDITS

Editors: Jo Finnis, Mark Bathurst, Will Steeds
Designer: Nigel Duffield
Typesetting: SX Composing Ltd, England
Color separation: Bantam Litho, England
Picture credits: All photographs by
  Bob Langrish, except for those on the
  following pages:
  Karine Devilder: 9; 10; 11; 12; 14; 16; 17; 18; 19;
  20; 21
  Tom and Doreen Bradley: 32 (top)
  Tish Quirk: 102 (bottom)
Indexer: Caroline Macy
Authenticator: Julia Longland

10 9 8 7 6 5 4 3 2 1

Printed in Italy

AUTHOR'S NOTE

I asked George Morris to assess the riders featured in this book because by any standards he is unique. He combines a deep fount of knowledge, practical ability and teaching prowess, and has been the most influential trainer in the United States for more than two decades – a situation which will no doubt prevail into the next century.

An international rider, George has a hunter-type forward seat which he has developed through an innate love of the French and Italian ideology of riding. He claims that this love is born of his temperament; although he is of German ancestry, he does not lean towards the Germanic principles.

CONTENTS

FOREWORD

There have been so many books written about show jumping over the years that it came as a refreshing surprise to find one with a completely new formula. What makes *The Masters of Show Jumping* so different is that it asks the most important people in the sport – the riders themselves – what they think. The riders' own comments on subjects ranging from their criteria for selecting horses to preferred training methods and, more generally, the 'state of the sport' are, usefully, given in the context of a brief history of the particular rider's background and development.

I first met the author of *The Masters of Show Jumping*, Ann Martin, at the New York Horse Show in Madison Square Garden. She was busy giving each of my team – who had just won the Nations' Cup – a huge celebratory chrysanthemum to wear in their buttonholes at the prize-giving ceremony on the last day of the show.

Since then, we have become firm friends, not least because of our shared interest in the sport. Show jumping is Ann's favourite equestrian discipline and, travelling the national and international circuits, she has come to know most of the riders featured in the book really well. This, coupled with her own love and knowledge of the horse, shows in her writing: the riders trust her, and have spoken very freely both of the disappointments and of the high points of their careers.

Ann's choice of the leading American trainer, George Morris, to analyse her chosen show jumpers' special qualities, meanwhile, was inspired, for George is both highly perceptive and eloquent in his comments.

Whether it be George's comments, Ann's knowledgeable writing and astute questions, or reading about a rider's most emotional moments (such as Joe Fargis's despair with Touch of Class before the start of the Los Angeles Olympic Games), the reader will find much of interest in *The Masters of Show Jumping* – be he or she an international, a novice or an armchair fan of the sport.

Ronnie Massarella

By Ronnie Massarella, O.B.E.,
Senior Manager of the British Show Jumping Team, 1970 –.

INTRODUCTION

Two of the aspects of international show jumping which fascinate me most are the kaleidoscope of styles displayed by the top competitors, and the different influences which have shaped those riders' various styles.

In Great Britain the sport is dominated by certain families, whose members have an innate understanding of the horse. The family of Welshman Fred Broome is one such dynasty: his son David, his daughter Liz and her husband Ted have all achieved many victories at the highest levels, while Ted and Liz's daughter Marie continued the family tradition by winning the European Young Riders Championship in 1990. Yorkshire, a county as renowned for its show jumpers as for its cricketers, offers similar examples of British show-jumping dynasties, with Harvey Smith and his sons Robert and Steven, and with John and Michael Whitaker. When, in August, 1989, the Whitaker brothers won their first major individual international honours (the gold and silver medals respectively at the European Championships in Rotterdam), the only surprise was that their talents had not been rewarded earlier.

The 1988 Olympic triumph of France's Pierre Durand and Jappeloup, meanwhile, epitomizes the heights that can be reached by a freak horse of outstanding scope and athleticism coupled with a hard-working rider with a brilliant brain.

Qualities shared by the leading Germans are strength, durability, superb basic groundwork and the ability to smile philosophically when the going gets tough.

In complete contrast to the Europeans, the United States teams are famed for their classical style, the roots of which evolved in the great pre-war cavalry schools. This is largely due to the influence of Bertalan de Nemethy, who became coach to the United States Equestrian Team (U.S.E.T.) in 1955.

In 1932, 'Bert', as he is affectionately known, was a Cavalry Lieutenant in the 3rd Hussars of Count Nadasdy at Sopron. After attending the Hungarian Cavalry School at Örkény-Tabor (south of Budapest) and then the German Cavalry School at Krampitz (Potsdam) he became an instructor, and jumped for the Hungarian team at events all over Europe. When World War II broke out, Bert crossed the Atlantic to the United States and took American citizenship.

As coach to the U.S.E.T., Bert laid the foundations of the U.S.'s current strength in depth, and his riders soon had a host of Nations' Cup and Grand Prix victories to their credit. Now retired, the legacy of Bert's training lives on in the style of those who rode on his teams.

Whatever national characteristics and stylistic influences the riders featured in *The Masters of Show Jumping* display, it is nevertheless still true that each of them has his or her own highly individual hallmark, whether it be a particular matter of style or in selection procedures.

By Ann Martin

PIERRE DURAND

Pierre is a worker but does not have quite the natural talent of some of the other most successful riders. In a way, he's rather like me because I'm a worker not a talent. He is an intelligent, very organized fellow and compensates for his lack of inherent talent with his brilliant brain and attitude towards work. Jappeloup is not an easy horse. I saw him first in his early days, when he stopped in the combinations at Longchamps because he did not realize his ability. He is not nearly as easy to produce as everyone thinks. On the day after the Nations' Cup at the Seoul Olympics in 1988, Pierre was out preparing for the individual competition doing gymnastic work with Jappeloup while almost everyone else was loafing around, so I have a great respect for him. As a teacher, I prefer a worker with an average talent to a talent who is an average worker. You very seldom get a rider who is both highly talented and hard working, as in the cases of Katie Monahan Prudent or Conrad Homfeld.

George Morris

When professional lawyer Pierre Durand touched his dream by adding the supreme accolade of the Olympic individual gold medal in Seoul, 1988, to his, and Jappeloup's, 1987 European Championship, even their severest critics conceded that luck had not played so much as a fleeting element in their success.

Their joint story embraces all the elements of a happy fairy-tale. Pierre began as an event rider, but a minor fall, then a subsequent fall and brief visit to hospital, upset his mother very much. Madame Durand remains so nervous of her son's equestrian exploits that she never attends a show or watches live coverage of her son competing. Conversely, Pierre's father, Serge Durand, the owner of a

tile-making factory in St Seurin sur L'Isle, is one of his son's most ardent supporters. Pierre's family has no equestrian background and Monsieur Durand's own sporting interest was football. Now he is president of the local *écurie* (riding school), in a section of which Pierre has five recently completed horse boxes in a beautifully restored cow byre.

The young Pierre was in no way deterred by his falls, and he happily switched his allegiance to show jumping to please his mother, although as recently as 1980 he had a good eventer and competed at top international competitions such as Pompadour. Earlier schooling from the former French international three day event rider, Dominic Bentejac, meant that his flat work and jumping were already above average. By 1971, he was regularly in the money.

In an age of increasing professionalism, one of the most remarkable features of Pierre's success at that time was the part-time status of his competitive career. An arrangement with the Business Tribunal which supplied much of his work allowed a 50-50 division of his time.

Show jumping took a back seat when Pierre spent four years at Bordeaux University,

Far left: Pierre and Jappeloup, at Aix-la-Chapelle (Aachen), negotiate a big vertical with considerable ease as part of their Olympic preparations in 1988. The permanent arena at Aix is among the world's best – and most exacting – and there is no more knowledgeable crowd.

Left: Pierre with Jappeloup (left) and Narcotique. Narcotique, who is by Selle Français stallion Fair Play out of an Anglo-Arab mare, possesses more strength and substance than this breeding would suggest. Pierre won the St Gallen Grand Prix on her in 1989, and the Newtron Masters in Amsterdam in 1990. "She not only has scope but an extremely level temperament."

graduating with a Masters degree in both law and political science. From there, he went on to run his own offices in Libourne, specializing in business bankruptcy.

Pierre first heard of Jappeloup when the horse was four years old. He went to see, but did not buy. "I did not want him. I was impressed but he was too thin and so little. I did not imagine that he could become so good and so fantastic," says Pierre. But Jappeloup – by the trotter Le Tyrol II, who was put down because he was thought to be no use as a stallion, out of a thoroughbred mare, Venerable – and Pierre were destined for each other. A year later, Pierre tried and bought the brown gelding. Although Jappeloup was very green, exploded over jumps and attempted two-stride doubles in one, Pierre rode him in one or two shows and Jappeloup put in a refusal now and then.

After patient schooling through their first winter together, then 20 shows in 1981, Pierre knew that his new partner would be at least very good if he were allowed to continue making progress in an unhurried fashion.

"From then on, the demands of my situation and business were Jappeloup's good

Above: The riding club at the village of Saint Seurin sur L'Isle. The local mayor has now added Pierre's Olympic title to the board. In the background, the indoor arena can be seen.

Right: Pierre's indoor stables at Saint Seurin are housed in an old farm building. The big golden-coloured bell hanging from the ceiling was awarded to Pierre when he won the individual European title in 1987.

The combination's success stems partly from the effort Pierre made, after his disaster at the Los Angeles Olympic Games, to understand his horse's weaknesses – not the approach to, but the actual technique of jumping, verticals. At the time, he consciously developed a 'softer seat'. "I now respond more sympathetically to Jappeloup. Our minds are better. We both have much more affinity with and confidence in each other than before."

Each month Jappeloup has a blood test and also an annual two-day full veterinary check when every inch is x-rayed. Two or three times a week between shows he is hacked out down the plane-tree-lined roads and through vineyards, fields of fat brown sheep and grey stone villages to give variety.

Pierre rates himself a self-made rider while attributing much of his success to his wife Nadia, who acts as groundsman. The couple, who married in 1981, have a daughter, Lisa, who is aged six. Their home is Le Grand Palat at St Emilion, nine miles away from the stables.

Nadia is the twin daughter of Patrick Devilder, who owns a cotton importing business in

Left: Pierre gives Jappeloup a change of scene as he rides through the vineyards which surround the riding school at Saint Seurin.

Below: Every morning when he is at home at Le Grand Palat, near St. Emilion, Pierre takes his daughter Lisa to school. Here, Nadia sees them off before leaving for her office, where she will prepare for her next auction.

luck. I was forced to work him slowly, take time and not overpressurize him. I was always interested in jumping and by then had enough time and experience to know just how to work horses." Jappeloup made his international debut at Longchamps. Barcelona and Madrid followed, and the gelding was now set on the path to supremacy.

Pierre considers that after riding the exceptional Jappeloup he will never experience quite the same pleasure with other horses. But he is sure that if Jappeloup had not been in his stables from the very beginning – rather in a professional yard and used too soon – he would not have been as good. "He needed a long time to understand how to jump. He is very careful, very brave, has big energy and is as supple as a cat."

Jappeloup is aloof, independent and a 'Garbo' of horses; he prefers to be alone. He never whinnies to another horse and hates loud music at shows. He is a good traveller – providentially, because the nearest international shows, apart from Bordeaux, are at least 600 miles (966km) away.

Right: When she was as young as
two years old (as here), Pierre
took daughter Lisa riding to
familiarize her with horses. Lisa
now rides her own pony.

Right: When she was as young as two years old (as here), Pierre took daughter Lisa riding to familiarize her with horses. Lisa now rides her own pony.

Lille. Her sister Karine is an equestrian journalist and photographer. Enterprisingly, Nadia trained as an auctioneer some eight years ago and now runs her own business. Nadia holds sales – "of cars, antiques, anything" – every Tuesday, so that she can travel to shows at weekends with Pierre.

SELECTION

Since Pierre was involved only part-time in show jumping before 1989, he had not bought many show jumpers. However, Jappeloup proved the ideal subject for a discussion of Pierre's priorities, which focus on the entire area behind the saddle.

He must have a horse with a strong back and loins, short behind the saddle with well-developed and muscled hindquarters; also long hind legs, especially the area between stifle and hocks, and the latter must be big, flat and clean.

"Unlike a kangaroo and all animals with natural jumping ability, to me a horse is not made to jump – a jumper is a special horse and he is not more aesthetic than a non-jumper. It doesn't matter to me if the horse's forehand is light and not very well developed. I like the horse to be powerful behind."

Jappeloup, who stands approximately 15.3 hands high, is higher behind than in front, so "He is not a very comfortable ride, but effective". However, he fulfils all his owner's requirements with his immensely powerful rear end. While showmen might criticize him for his lighter front, long legs and the fact that he is not deep of girth, they cannot deny that he is the most proven of flying machines.

The dark brown gelding's other assets include short cannon bones and a dense flat bone. Jappeloup was foaled in 1975 and, unusually, bears no signs of wear and tear. When aged 14 in August 1989, he was, as his owner–rider succinctly said, "Young in heart and body, *un jeune homme*".

He has the wide forehead that typifies an intelligent horse, honest open eyes, and is very alert and interested. Constantly pricking his ears, he is aware he is king of his own domain, and although he is independent by nature, he has a very close affinity and good relationship with Pierre and is clearly always delighted to see him in the stable.

What, I asked, of the crucial element of temperament? "The horse must have a fair outlook, be straight and honest. He should be able to accept a lot of work and the total authority of the rider."

Jappeloup has a big personality and a strong character. "He is very willing to go but doesn't like authority. With him, I must use diplomacy. But, when I am ready for a big event, he is always responding, always I can count on the fact that if I am ready, he is. He is devoted to me, his rider, providing I ask the right question at the right time. He gives with great generosity.

"As far as action is concerned, again I look to see how the horse walks behind. If the imprint of the back hoof is in front of that of the front hoof, it means the horse is very engaged, and the horse must pull in a straight line when pushing forward." The imprint of Jappeloup's hind hoof is nine inches [23cm] in front of his front hoof.

"Suppleness is essential and size doesn't matter, but I prefer little horses because I find they adapt more easily and tend to be more naturally supple and agile than larger ones."

He prefers to buy a horse aged from four to six years old, when the animal has already done some jumping and is ready to go on.

TRAINING

Pierre's schooling at the crucial initial stage of moulding a partnership was extremely effective – so much so, that in a mere two years, Jappeloup was competing at his first international show.

At first Pierre concentrated on developing cadence through work at a very slow pace to try to get Jappeloup much more engaged. He concentrated on getting the horse's back legs under him. At shows, he hacks Jappeloup to calm him down, to make him settled and re-laxed, no matter what the situation or place. He then works him technically.

Pierre later progressed Jappeloup on to grids – a series of low jumps, sometimes with definite jump-off poles, with one, two or more strides between them. As it was intended, this controlled jumping gradually improved Jap-peloup's trajectory. His high knee action, in-herited from his *trotteur* sire, ensured that he would seldom touch a fence in front. But he had so much inherent power that at doubles he frequently threw such a big jump that he landed at the foot of the next jump with scant chance of clearing it, and a knock-down or re-fusal was the only possible outcome. But, with continued grid work and patience, Jap-peloup gradually learnt how to control his enormous natural jump.

The type of bridle that Jappeloup wore at the Olympic Games in Seoul evolved through a variety of experiences over the years. Originally he was ridden in a double but gradually Pierre became aware that Jappe-loup was tending to lean too much on the bit. Because of the risk involved in making a major bridle change immediately before an important competition, Pierre waited until after the World Championships at Aix-la-Chapelle (the French name for the German town of Aachen) in 1986.

There, despite the fact that the double bridle was no longer satisfactory, the pair were leading on points before the contro-versial four-rider jump-off, in which con-tenders ride their own and each other's horses – a formula that may entertain the crowd but is not favoured by the majority of the leading international riders as the decider for such a coveted title. They finished in fourth place behind Canada's Gail Green-ough, Conrad Homfeld of the United States and Britain's Nick Skelton.

Another reason Pierre changed bridles was "to improve my equitation". With a broken pelham, Pierre has retained the same authority but with the use of much less force. Jappeloup is much lighter on the bit. "It is a more subtle form of power."

Other refinements include a leather curb strap, which is far gentler in action than the more usual chain of metal links. The top rein

Below: Pierre and Jappeloup give a jump ample clearance at Hickstead in 1985. When Pierre was training him, one problem was how to control Jap's strength, to prevent him over-jumping and thus landing too near the next fence.

Right: Pierre has introduced various refinements to Jappeloup's bridle over a period of time. As seen here, the two reins are linked together on each side, and the wide curb strap is made of leather.

Below: Pierre and Jappeloup return across the empty sands with Nadia and the speed horse Sunfly after an early morning exercise session on the beach at Le Touquet. Variety of work is an integral part of success for Pierre.

has a rubber grip, "to get a good catch and not disturb the horse if I get things wrong".

While competing in the Zürich Grand Prix in July 1988, Pierre's chance of victory evaporated in the jump-off when he lost the bottom rein and experienced much difficulty regaining it. After that, he connected the two reins by means of leather straps 2in (5cm) long, each attached to the reins by two rings. If ever he loses the lower rein, he is now able to retrieve it far more quickly.

It is the art of the show jumper to stand back and coolly assess his horse's attributes and defects. Much of Pierre's success is attributable to the way he has studied and analysed Jappeloup's strengths and weaknesses, working hard on improving the latter.

Jap's good qualities include being quick in both action and reaction; he listens and responds to his rider at all times. His courage is boundless, he senses and rises to a big occasion and he is strong both mentally and physically. At the end of 1988, it was Pierre's pride that "In all his career, he has never been unable to work, for even a day".

As for weaknesses one problem was the fact that just before a jump Jappeloup did not always lift his legs high enough.

Another weakness which has been diminished is Jappeloup's tendency to get too much weight forward on to his shoulders just before take-off, thereby affecting his *trajectoire*. This was remedied, as described earlier, by grid work and work on the flat to get him better balanced and his hind legs under him.

A further problem was that his technique at verticals was often bad. Pierre notes, "He now approaches verticals quite differently, in a more collected style which he has achieved through grid work. Jappeloup is never jumped high or often in training, and each jump is a clever, well-thought-out one, designed to teach him something special."

Meanwhile, Pierre has improved his seat to become softer and more sympathetic than before. "I now disturb him less because I have taught myself to be discreet and quieter; this means I get a better attitude from Jap."

The Olympic champion has also learnt that "Even on 'D Day', I must never ask him to do something he is not ready to do. Basically it's to avoid psychological annoyance. That explains why so often I don't try to win a jump-off during my competitive training schedule in the weeks before my immediate target. I believe it is not helpful towards achieving my main aim."

Each year Pierre selects one or two main targets and then he plans the best preparation in order to be in peak form on the big day. He regards all the courses he tackles beforehand as a training ground to improve and tune-up either himself and/or his horse. "Such competitions provide time and the opportunity to achieve great harmony. It is easier to reach your horse's optimum when you have asked for less at the preceding events. Following this policy means the horse is much more likely to give of his best on the big day."

THE MAKING OF A CHAMPION

To rise from the dust and ashes of bitter disappointment at the Los Angeles Olympiad in 1984 to capture the supreme accolade of an individual gold medal at the following Olympics at Seoul in 1988 was a remarkable feat demanding a rare blend of courage, resolve and skill.

Above: Jappeloup has a strong and independent nature but, as this picture of him and Pierre clearing a jump at Aix in 1987 shows, he trusts Pierre and recognizes his authority.

Although Pierre's friend and team-mate Frédéric Cottier rode his very genuine Flambeau in three Olympics – the alternative Games in Rotterdam in 1980, Los Angeles and Seoul – at 17 years old Flambeau was a shadow of his former self in Korea. He was, however, still good enough to contribute to France's winning of the team bronze medals. Also, in recent years, only a small percentage of horses has taken part in even two Olympic Games.

Jappeloup was only nine years old in Los Angeles, but the demands of show jumping in the past decade have increased dramatically with the development of a permanent European winter indoor circuit, putting increased stress on the horses, few of whom now enjoy the benefit of a complete and relaxing break from the sport.

The gelding's soundness and Pierre's firm refusal to overcampaign him were strong contributory factors towards Jappeloup's Olympic reappearance at his peak in Seoul. The key factor in Pierre's Los Angeles problems was that the Games fell at the end of what was both his and Jappeloup's second only international season.

As a relatively new international rider, Pierre was not sufficiently confident and had not been free to prepare as he had wanted for the great Olympic challenge, his most important assignment ever. This was because Marçel Rozier was the national team trainer at the time, which meant that Pierre was not able to follow his own very individual training methods as he wished.

To succeed as a largely self-taught rider, Pierre needed to continue his own highly personalized, independent and, to some degree, unorthodox preparations. But, at this stage of his career, "I doubted the verity of my methods and found myself between two waters. My confidence was at a low ebb because I had not achieved sufficiently good results to confirm to myself that, for Jappeloup, my methods were right."

At Los Angeles, Pierre's acid test came in the second round of the Prix des Nations, the team competition in which he was jumping last instead of in his usual second or third position. In the first round he had 8 faults and then needed a clear round for the French team to secure the bronze medal.

"The pressure on me was too great at the time," he recalled. "My problem came at the ninth fence, the *barrière* [gate]. It was dark and narrow. At the time Jappeloup didn't like such obstacles and he was afraid. As we approached I did not have him sufficiently

collected and his take-off stride was too big. The jump went all wrong, I was shot to the ground and France's medal hopes were lost."

Pierre managed to finish a creditable fourteenth in the individual competition, which, if not as high a placing as he had hoped, at least served to restore some of his confidence.

As he is his own severest critic and a self-made rider, the following weeks were inevitably dominated by an analysis of his Olympic performance.

His wife Nadia gave him solid, unswerving and valuable support in his plan to continue his methods in the future. The multi-talented rider and trainer, Nelson Pessoa, helped him for a short while during this critical period, and the Frenchman received from him a

Above right: Pierre jumping Narcotique at home. The mare has much potential, but gives a very different type of ride to Jappeloup. Although Pierre has already won a Grand Prix on her, wisely he is allowing himself time to establish a partnership with Narcotique.

Right: Pierre talks to the French television commentator Jean Marquet after walking the Grand Prix course at Aix. To help him concentrate before important classes, Pierre listens to music on his personal cassette player seen here fixed to his belt.

piece of vital and timely advice when he summed up, "Don't change the way you ride; just alter some minor details".

It was a hard way to learn but, in retrospect, the catastrophic fall and resulting elimination helped Pierre's future progress. Pierre now feels the failure made him work all the harder to improve.

From his results in the ensuing years up to Seoul it was apparent that Pierre and Jappeloup were in the ascendancy. At the major championships their placings were:

1985 World Cup Final, Berlin: **3rd**
European Championships, Dinard
Individual: **9th**
1986 World Cup Final, Gothenburg: **11th**
World Championships, Aix-la-
Chapelle (Aachen)
Individual: **4th**
Team: **3rd**
1987 World Cup Final, Bercy, Paris: **7th**
European Championships, St Gallen
Individual: **1st**
Team: **2nd**
1988 World Cup Final, Gothenburg: **2nd**
1989 European Championships, Rotterdam
Individual: **4th**
Team: **2nd**
1990 World Cup Final, Dortmund: **2nd**
World Championships, Stockholm
Team: **1st**

The acid test came on the last morning of the 1988 Olympic Games, the day of the individual finals. In Seoul, on the morning of Sunday, 2 October, 1988, Pierre and Nadia Durand woke early. Pierre was in good humour, his only flash of annoyance being at the late arrival of breakfast. Nadia, the archetypal show-jumping wife, all too well aware of the vital role of verbal punch-ball she must sometimes, and then most importantly, play, wisely held her tongue and did not answer back. She recalls, "Inevitably, the pressure was enormous. So, I had to do everything I could to ensure as calm a start as possible for the big day so that Pierre could concentrate 100 per cent on the task ahead of him."

Although the statement a friend had made to Pierre before he left for Korea kept winging across her mind, she kept cool and betrayed no outward sign of her thoughts. The words

of the statement were, "Every 12 years, the French show jumpers bring home a gold medal. Pierre Jonquères d'Oriola from Helsinki in 1952 and again from Tokyo in 1964, then the team gold medals from Montreal in 1976." The pattern was there; would it, could it, continue?

At 6.00 a.m. precisely, the chauffeur of the minibus was waiting in reception to drive them in the dark through the wide deserted avenues from the Olympic Village to the stables. The horses, too, had had an unusually early start and were in the proccss of being unloaded from the horse boxes that had brought them to the main Olympic Stadium in the centre of Seoul from their Olympic base at Kwachon.

Pierre walked down the double line of covered temporary boxes searching for Jappeloup, who had been one of the first to arrive. He relaxed when he found the gelding enjoying a roll in the deep fresh straw of his box.

The hours before a major contest can all too easily hang heavy as the tension swiftly rises. As so often before, Pierre busied himself by giving his boots a final polish to calm himself and to give his groom, Bernadette, as much time as possible to concentrate on Jappeloup's preparation.

He noticed with pleasure that on the belt of her jeans Bernadette was wearing a small crocheted hat. Just before he had won the European title at St Gallen in 1987, an old invalid lady who lived in a small Swiss village

Left: The two Pierres meet at Saint Seurin following the 1988 Olympics. Pierre Jonquères d'Oriola (left), Olympic champion in 1952 and 1964, congratulates Pierre Durand – the first Frenchman to emulate his feat. *"Bravo, Pierre, maintenant nous sommes deux!"*

Right: Nadia attends shows with Pierre whenever her business and looking after their daughter Lisa permit. Here, the couple enjoy a joke together before Pierre's defence of his title at Rotterdam in 1989.

Below right: Pierre and Jappeloup in 1988, during one of the qualifying classes at Kwachon prior to the individual final held in the Olympic Stadium, Seoul.

Anita four years before, Pierre was mentally strong and quietly confident that, granted the essential element of luck, he and Jappeloup were tuned for the optimum occasion and ready to take on the best in the world and to show they could reign supreme.

Following the trend set by Bertalan de Nemethy, the architect of the Los Angeles Olympics who drew most successfully on California as a theme for his courses, Petersen's jumps were a spectacular interpretation of the culture of Korea, of which he had made a very comprehensive study.

Petersen's challenge was one for which Pierre felt well equipped. Games prior to Los Angeles had put a premium on power – de Nemethy heralded and spearheaded a change in course construction that Petersen both supported and developed. The West German demanded of competitors the ability to master a highly technical course. If all went smoothly, a very well-schooled horse with a

had given him a similar good luck symbol. During 1988, Madam Paulette Anthony had made a new *porte bonheur* for Pierre with the Games expressly in mind, which he had given to Bernadette. Now at the crucial moment it reassured him to see her wearing it.

Overnight the German course designer, Olaf Petersen, had supervised the construction of the 15-fence track on which he had long worked. Dawn had only just broken and the spotlights were still on when, at 7.00 a.m. precisely, the arena was opened for the course walk and the 37 qualified riders, accompanied by their trainers, *chef d'équipes* and entourages, poured across the green carpet and over the red running track on to the wide-leaved, oriental grass on which the obstacles were sited.

Pierre was jostling shoulders with the riders he feared most: Canada's 1988 Volvo World Cup *vainqueurs*, Ian Millar and Big Ben; West Germany's Franke Sloothaak and Walzerkönig; and three Americans – the defending champion Joe Fargis (with Mill Pearl), Greg Best (with Gem Twist) and Anne Kursinski (with Starman), who were to finish second and fourth equal respectively, separated by the wild card, Germany's Karsten Huck with Nepomuk. However, in total contrast to the equivalent competition at Santa

sound, basic dressage training, an athletic horse with a good technique and obviously Olympic scope, would come out on top.

"If I had one personal criticism," says Pierre, "it was that time was short for me and you could not choose your route. It was all dictated – there were no optional routes to fences, no chance to cut shorter to get inside the time limit."

Time was uppermost in Pierre's mind because in the team competition the combination had incurred one time fault in the first round, prior to their second round clear which had clinched the team bronze medals for France.

As Pierre watched the earlier horses tackle the course he formed no special strategy but worried about the wavy planks. "Planks are never easy. For Jap and me the problem was magnified because the planks were narrow and the middle of the fence the highest." However, despite his rider's misgivings, Jap jumped the fence well.

On a more personal note, Pierre received a completely unexpected and most welcome psychological boost when Bill Steinkraus, winner of the individual gold medal for the United States on Snowbound at Mexico in 1968, slipped up to him after the course walk, holding a piece of paper.

"Keep this with you this morning," he counselled, putting the paper into Pierre's hand. "It will bring you good fortune." And Bill was gone, as silently as he had come, his mission discreetly and delicately achieved.

Pierre opened his hand and found an old dollar bill, which he carries with him to this day. Soon afterwards he experienced infinite pleasure as he mounted Jappeloup. The sun was rising, there were no technical problems ahead that he felt were insurmountable. He decided to go for a faultless round and not worry unduly about the clock.

Many floundered at the astonishing water combination complex – fences at which water almost surrounded the approach, with the entrance guarded by huge and exotic oriental birds. Jap, however, simply tucked up his legs very tightly and, sensing the importance of the occasion, took even more care than he usually does.

After the first round Karsten Huck, who had watched from the sidelines while his German

compatriots won the team gold medals, held a slender lead with the only faultless round on Nepomuk. Pierre was second with 0.25 time faults and Ian Millar hard on his heels, far too close for comfort with 0.75. Other competitors were still very much in touch on four faults.

In the second round the riders jumped in reverse order of merit, which meant that Pierre was second last. He was by no means disheartened and said to Patrick Caron, "The pressure will be on Huck, he is not used to that". With half an hour's break while the course was altered, Pierre sat down alone, preparing for the ultimate challenge. He listened to music from some of his favourite tapes, preparing for the following round.

Patrick came and ended Pierre's private reverie; the final course walk was about to begin. The fences were big and demanding but not impossible. There were some very testing distances demanding maximum extension and then immediate shortening, which heightened their hopes because Jappeloup now excelled at this type of test.

As Pierre watched the first horse go in to jump, his old friend, Frédéric Cottier, stood alongside him, and together they considered the technical opportunities that the course presented.

Above: Pierre and Jappeloup – his ears pricked attentively forward – at Kwachon in the second round of the 1988 Olympic team show-jumping competition, when their immaculate clear round secured the bronze medals for France.

Above: A dream that few show jumpers have the chance to realize: Pierre, on the victory rostrum at Seoul in 1988, kisses the coveted gold medal.

Pierre calmed Jap and, precisely as the bell rang, he was on his way. He had the horse's entire concentration, with a resultant clear round and one time fault.

The Frenchman's destiny now rested entirely in the hands of Karsten Huck. He stood with Patrick Caron, his team partners Frédéric, Michel Robert and Hubert Bourdy, and his father. The tension was so unbearable that Pierre turned away, unable to watch the deciding round. Then he heard a pole hit the ground – the first part of the seventh, a double, had come down.

After a long embrace with Nadia, his colleagues and team mates lifted him shoulder high in triumph. The destiny of the gold medal was now known. Pierre had deservedly won the highest honour the sport has to offer. Huck had to be satisfied with the bronze medal after a two-horse jump-off with America's Greg Best on Gem Twist, who claimed the silver.

Deliriously happy, Pierre's first words were, "Few men are as fortunate as I have been today because I have touched my dream. I wish I could cut the medal in half and share it with Jappeloup."

EPILOGUE

Prior to the Prix des Nations in Seoul, Pierre surprised me by saying he was seriously considering giving up show jumping if he were fortunate enough to win the individual gold medal. He explained, "I would rather give up at the top than continue as Jappeloup's physical ability gradually decreases with age. I do not want the image of Jap to deteriorate, and that is a big risk if I go on too long."

Press Conference

Pierre is facing a packed press room at the Bordeaux International Horse Show, in December, 1988. At his side is Patrick Proisy, the Paris-based General Manager of Mark McCormack's International Management Group in France.

"I have asked you to come because I have considered deeply whether to continue or stop taking part in my sport. It has been difficult to decide but I have come down in favour of the former. I would have liked to have

Back in Jap's saddle, only one doubt remained for the rider, possessed as he is of a sharp brain, an intellectual rather than an instinctive rider. Should he go in front of or behind the massive bed of flowers which preceded the combination? The more testing, former route would save time.

No stone was left unturned. As a final precaution after his last warm-up jumps, Pierre sent Bernadette running to the stables for a pot of petroleum jelly. With the help of Biscotte, reserve rider Philippe Rozier's groom, the front of Jappeloup's legs, from knees and hocks to hooves, were smeared with grease so that if they touched a jump they would, it was hoped, slide over the pole rather than topple it with the friction.

Ian Millar and Big Ben preceded Pierre. This time they cracked, totalling 12.25 penalties for a disappointing final 15th place.

stopped after the Olympic Games because for me that is the supreme accolade; no other is comparable.

"I wanted to be the Olympic champion. *J'ai caressé cette rêve*. But, my sporting life is not in harmony with my work. There is no plasmosis." He added, jokingly, "I have had some discussions with Jap, and he said that we should continue to compete against John Whitaker and Milton.

"For three reasons, I am going to give up my work as a lawyer and continue jumping. Now that I am the Olympic champion so many new opportunities have opened for me. Secondly, all being well, Jappeloup should have two more years of top-level international competition in him; and finally, as my example of promotion I take the skier Jean-Claude Killy. I see my future progress going that way, it is the logical development, so I called in someone with the necessary *savoir faire*. By my standards I cannot win more, but I will continue because in life it is necessary to be realistic. Now, I have such a good solution and change in life that I have no option but to continue."

Under the rules of the International Olympic Association, Pierre retained his amateur status. His gold-medal victory brought in many lucrative proposals, and he determined to make the most of them in the years leading up to the 1992 Olympiad and also had several separate advertising endorsements.

Previously he had not had time for back-up horses but he planned to enlarge his stable with the acquisition of two or three more Grand Prix calibre horses. The first were Narcotique, an 11-year-old Selle Français mare and Pin Pin du Valon. "Now I have changed my philosophy and approach, my strategy is to develop a good PR image through first-class promotion."

The 1989 Volvo World Cup Final in Tampa, Florida, was not a major target. One reason for this was that Jappeloup is a carrier of paraplasmosis, for which there is a quarantine in Florida.

For Jappeloup, Pierre envisaged one or two main objectives each year. For 1989 his European title defence was the priority. "It would be sporting to defend my title."

Adjusting to the demands of increased sponsorship proved testing in 1989. By then,

Pierre was also a member of the two-man Team Renault with his Olympic bronze-medal-winning colleague Michel Robert.

Because of his new association with Renault, Pierre, who prefers to prepare Jap for competition with a fairly light pre-show schedule, had to add Cannes and Franconville in France and Kapellen in Belgium to his preparation shows as they staged Renault Jump Grand Prix.

All in all, 1989 proved to be a season of acclimatization for Pierre. Riding for the first time as a full-time competitor, he not only received an increasing number of invitations to compete, but also – because of his Olympic success – experienced the pressure of being introduced as the champion.

Overall, it was not a vintage season. In August at the European Championships in Rotterdam, Pierre and Jappeloup finished sixth, losing their European title to John Whitaker and Milton. However, at the World Championships in Stockholm in 1990 Pierre and Jappeloup were members of the French team who won the team gold medal.

Pierre finally decided to retire Jappeloup from championship, Nations' Cup and Grand Prix competition after the 1990 Bordeaux World Cup, while he was still at the top. He plans some guest appearances for Jap at smaller events in 1991 "if he feels well and sound, so that his public can see him".

Below: Pierre at work in his office. Pierre used to specialize in business bankruptcy cases but in 1988, after his Olympic success, he took the decision to concentrate on show jumping full-time.

JOHN WHITAKER

John is one of the greatest riders seen in this or any era. He is calm and quiet with tremendous horse sense and has obviously grown up with horses and horse people. He thinks horse and has as great a pair of hands as I've ever seen in my life. Think of smooth riders with whom he's comparable, like Conrad Homfeld and Katie Monahan Prudent. The total efficiency of all three gives results in both Grand Prix and Speed Classes. If I were compiling a list of the top ten riders of the century, John would be on it. There is not a better rider in the world today.

George Morris

As the British Number One with an official points-ranking over 100 per cent ahead of his nearest rival, his brother Michael, John Whitaker does not have to go out looking for horses. "You can travel miles searching for them and find nothing. They just turn up out of the blue," he says with typical modesty.

SELECTION

There is no set type of horse that John searches for. He feels that it is so hard to find a good horse that "One can't be too choosy about type. Gammon is the nearest to my type in my present string because he is similar to Ryan, both in his characteristics and the way he goes."

Gammon, who was foaled in 1979, is an Oldenburg gelding by Goldpitz and was sent to John to try by the German dealer Axel Wockener, who thought that the gelding would suit him. Liz Edgar's former multi-winning partner, Everest Forever, was bought from the same source.

The gelding is quite sharp, active and forward going, and because John evolved and developed his style round Ryan in his formative years, he finds Gammon easier to ride than Hopscotch or Milton.

When trying a horse, John rides it if it is broken. Otherwise he puts his possible purchase over a jump in the loose school. Most of the horses he is sent are usually too green to do very much and he therefore rates their attitude to jumping, how they canter and their balance as very important at this stage.

He finds it hard to assess how careful a horse is at this time but considers it most important later on.

His preference is for a 16.1 hands high horse, 16.2 hands high at the most, mainly because he is not very big himself. (He measures 5ft 8in (1.7m) tall and is of slight build.) If a horse is over 16.2 hands high, he finds it difficult to control properly. However, it must be big enough to cope with long distances and big fences.

Now that his international season lasts ten months each year and he is constantly travelling, John does not have the time he would like to spend with the real youngsters; so, although he makes exceptions, he is

Far left: Poise, balance and confidence are combined as John and Ryan's Son commence their descent of the Derby Bank at Hickstead. They won the Hickstead Derby in 1983.

Below: The Whitaker family ride out together at Heyside Farm. From left to right are Clare (on Hopscotch), Robert (on Sioux City), Louise (on Pipsqueak) and John (on Henderson Milton).

Above: John training on Gammon at home. Gammon missed most of the 1990 season due to a variety of health problems, including travel sickness.

now Milton. He reflects on their similarities and assets and how he adapted from Ryan to the very different Milton.

When Mr and Mrs Tom Bradley offered John the ride on Milton, he felt it was a great compliment, although in the interim at another stable, since their daughter Caroline's untimely death, Milton had not fulfilled his potential. Nevertheless, he was already among the élite of the future.

On account of his type and the way he went, Milton was a totally different proposition from Ryan's Son, the horse on whom John had formed his style as the pair learnt together and battled their way to the Number One British rating. By nature of his build, Ryan's stride was relatively shorter than that of Milton, and he did not have as much natural ability. However, he completely compensated for these differences by virtue of his tremendous heart and the way in which he tackled every obstacle.

It is to John's eternal credit that, since he took over the ride on Milton, he has radically changed his style by shortening his stirrups and learning to sit back and wait for the grey, whose longer, loping stride presents his rider with a totally different challenge.

When Milton arrived at Heyside Farm in April, 1985, he was "so fat and unfit that I didn't jump him until the Rotherham Show the following September. I was lucky that Milton had a wonderful start with his groundwork with Caroline. It could not have been better." Caroline excelled in this department, having been taught the basics by the Swedish trainer Lars Sederholm.

John's immediate problem was that when Milton was with the rider who followed Caroline, he sustained an injury in the stable to his off-fore which was to keep him out of competition for nearly 18 months.

Prior to Rotherham, Milton had done two months' groundwork ("not that he needed it") interspersed with fittening hacks out – walking and trotting up the steep slopes of the surrounding Pennine Hills. "He was so very fat that I had to be extremely careful and go slowly and not damage his now recovered leg through the excess weight he carried.

"When I take on a fresh horse, I get on, ride it and see what happens. They usually listen more in the early stages of the partnership

basically more interested in unspoiled five- or six-year-olds that have already done some basic groundwork.

He rates the chestnut San Salvador, who joined his string in 1983, the year his son Robert was born, as his best speed horse ever. The Argentinian thoroughbred had more than 70 wins and two Rover cars to his credit by December 1990.

"Speed horses must be exceptionally careful because it is hard to keep them going, jumping fast and cleanly week after week." The finely built Salvador stands 16.1 hands high, the perfect size for John.

RYAN'S SON AND MILTON

Few show-jumping riders are fortunate enough to have one great horse in their lifetime. John Whitaker, who is only in his mid thirties, has already had two – Ryan's Son and

and react quicker. It is not until later, when the horse knows you, that you find the best way to ride him."

Basically, Milton is quite strong and powerful. In the early days, John's biggest problem was that Milton's stride was so long that the grey found short distances especially difficult. However, by 1989 "he was coping quite well. It wasn't a serious problem. I find it better to keep problems at the back of my mind, as I did then. If you make them too big a thing, you worry and can all too easily make the situation worse." John worked at shortening Milton's stride on the flat, thus developing the ability to get him in closer to a fence so that he picked up better in front. Despite Milton's huge ability, in his early days with John he could all too easily get caught out at "a pokey little stile after giving wide clearance to a preceding oxer". John has gradually improved Milton's technique at verticals. "I can make him use himself better when he stands off, giving him time to come up in front. In general I come in closer, but I have to be careful not to frighten him."

Verticals in front and short-distanced doubles, especially those with verticals out, remain his most vulnerable fences. But "The more you ride, the more you know what to do. Milton is basically careful, but any horse can be lazy and forgetful. My job is to know at which jump, and how, to help out my horses more than usual." At first, Milton sometimes jumped so high that he caught the back bar of an oxer with his hind legs as he came down.

There were of course disappointments in his progress, but John is nothing if not philosophical and the good days by far exceeded the bad. In autumn 1985, John took Milton to his first international, at Berlin, more for experience than anything else, and started him in the small classes, "which he enjoyed. His ears were pricked all the time." By the end of the show he had finished an encouraging third in the small Grand Prix.

The following week, he was second to Peter Charles and April Sun in the Brussels World Cup Qualifier and then travelled south to capture the Bordeaux equivalent. The partnership was being successfully established and cemented, and Milton was beginning to realize his tremendous ability – and to assume his correct place in the equestrian hierarchy.

John decided to jump Hopscotch in the 1986 World Championships at Aachen rather than Milton. It remains a decision he regrets, not because Hopscotch became upset and refused, but because afterwards, with the advantage of hindsight, he came to the conclusion that Milton could have coped with the courses with ease.

Left: Milton relaxing in the field at home – and spooking at a football. Note the protective bandages on his front legs.

Right: John on Hopscotch at Hickstead, 1985: "Hopscotch jumps very well at Hickstead, and has had many fine results there over the years".

Below: Hopscotch at the World Championships, Aachen, 1986 – one of those rare days when everything went wrong.

"Before, I wasn't too keen on jumping him because, although he'd gone well in Grand Prix, he still tended to overjump his fences and I thought that if we met anything big or complicated, we could well be in trouble. It wasn't worth rushing him at that stage; a set-back could have put him back a couple of years. Afterwards I thought I was perhaps wrong. Milton could have managed all the courses well, but I have no one to blame but myself. It was my decision."

"How would you rate Milton's intelligence?", I asked.

"I haven't yet figured out if a good international horse has a lot of intelligence or not, but Milton appears to have a lot. He's the type of horse who knows just how much he can get away with, how much he can push his luck with different people.

"My groom, Mandy, who is completely responsible for looking after him, can be a little bit soft and spoil him. Milton has sensed this and, for example, at a show before a jump-off when I'm studying the course, he'll walk just so far with her round the collecting ring, then he'll stop and refuse to take another step."

At the 1987 Royal Winter Fair in Toronto, the British horses were stabled on a second higher level, reached by a ramp. One day, Milton would not let Mandy lead him down and "I was walking the course and had to be found quickly to come and sort him out. I rode him down.

"He hates having his tail pulled. That's my wife Clare's responsibility – she's very good at smartening up the horses. We stand Milton on the other side of a solid and thick wooden half-door. If not, he would kick out and could well smash one of Clare's legs. If you gave up halfway through, you'd never do it again. You have to press on."

Milton's regular training pattern is designed to keep him competition fit, and he is seldom jumped at home. Usually only when he has had a long rest is he put over a few small fences, often at a small show like Markfield in Leicestershire. Every day he is hacked on the roads for 45 minutes to an hour. When the weather is good he is given a few hours in the field.

Milton was hob-dayed [an operation to improve a horse's breathing] before he came to John. Once a week, he is ridden to a nearby field where there is a quarter-mile gallop, which is ideal to give him a pipe-opener at three-quarter speed to keep him straight in his wind.

John finds it preferable to keep Milton in some degree of work during the short off-season because it takes him so long to get him back to peak condition. His longest rest is between the pre-Christmas Show at Olympia in London and the opening show of the following European World Cup qualifying series in late February.

The Irish-bred Ryan's Son was honoured by seven awards from the now defunct Irish Horse Board for the best competition horse of the year. They claimed he was by the stallion Ozymandias – a fact that John doubts because he has never seen any written proof. Nevertheless, the name fitted well enough because Ozymandias was a 'King of Kings' and Ryan was surely a king of Europe's show-jumping arenas for over a decade.

John's production of Ryan was in complete contrast to that of Milton, first and foremost because Ryan was so different, and secondly because John was inexperienced at the time. Plenty of trial, and sometimes error, were inevitable as they both learned and competed together. At this time, Ryan's tremendous temperament and courage extracted them from many tight corners.

Ryan did not have scope to burn but he gave all he had all the time and was very careful. His second, much anticipated Grade A season turned out to be one of his worst. This was because John didn't really know how to handle the horse that he now felt certain was a future star. "I didn't know then what I know now. I wrapped him up in cotton wool and fed him all too well over the winter of 1973–4, and he just wasn't the same all the next season. I had learnt the hard way never to let him get so big and overweight again."

In 1975, when Ryan was right physically, his jockey occasionally found him "too strong at some stages". Ever since Ryan had been there, John had ridden him in the bit in which he arrived, an old twisted snaffle with cheek pieces with one cheek piece missing.

John decided to experiment and tried a variety of bits, but none made any difference to his control. He returned, therefore, to the original bit, gave Ryan less energizing food

and did more school work to improve his control. Ryan was jumped in the same bit for the rest of his life. The bit was buckled to his bridle and the sides were regularly changed round.

After his trial-and-error bit sessions, the only changes John made were to Ryan's noseband. He was sometimes jumped in a crossed and sometimes a straight noseband.

In 1987, after Ryan's death, the sculptress Caroline Wallace was commissioned to make a lasting tribute in memory of the gallant Ryan. It was to be presented annually to the person who had contributed most to the sport each year. The British Team Manager, Ronnie Massarella, was chosen to be the first recipient; but, unfortunately, Caroline had cast a plain snaffle and after John had seen and admired the bronze, a hurried alteration had to be made before the award ceremony at Olympia.

Milton's assets include the fact that, just like Ryan, he rises to the occasion, whereas many other horses fall apart under pressure. "Milton is not the world's fastest, but his fantastic scope means that I can turn him into big fences as I do a speed horse over much smaller courses, and that is where he makes time. Six feet is as easy as three feet. He is basically careful."

Above: Ryan's Son jumping the planks at Hickstead: "In his long career, Ryan jumped against a lot of good horses, including Boomerang, St James, Philco, Sportsman, Deister, Jappeloup and Anglezarke. And he beat them all."

Right: John with Ryan's Son: "There was nowhere that Ryan didn't jump well. He was so consistent and he always tried hard, no matter what the show or ground."

Far right: Milton jumping at Hickstead, 1986. "He is plaited up here, which shows off his neck and crest. But he shakes his head because he doesn't like plaits, so we don't do it anymore."

He is a good traveller and when away from home, eats well and lies down to sleep. John will never forget the first jump he had on Milton after riding and working him on the flat for four months. "I jumped crossed poles and got the most tremendous feeling. Until that moment, I didn't realize what I had been missing. In some ways Milton is a freak; he jumps differently from any other horse I've ever ridden. It is the way he comes off the floor and lands. He is so light and smooth and easy."

Some horses grunt on landing after a jump because they are struggling. Milton jumps the biggest fences and lands as though he has just been cantering. "I've never felt I had to struggle on Milton and in some ways he's braver than Ryan was. Milton has only stopped once with me and that was in the Bordeaux World Cup Qualifier in 1988 because I misjudged a jump-off distance. You can ask him the impossible and he'll have a go. Ryan did know his limits but I can't remember him ever failing to reach a jump-off."

Right: Milton peers over his stable door. John and Michael signed a three-year contract with the Henderson Unit Trust in January 1990 and now all their horses jump with the Henderson prefix.

Milton has a great trust in John, which boosts John's confidence and is a crucial element in his ongoing success. The feeling is reciprocated because, John says, "When I walk a course that I am about to jump on Milton and hear the other riders' comments on the fences and how they intend to tackle them, I realize that to a large degree you rate a course by the horse power under you and know how lucky I am to have Milton".

Ryan's Hickstead Derby and King George V Gold Cup win at Britain's Royal International Horse Show are the successes that have meant most to John – the former because the Derby at Douglas Bunn's Hickstead arena is held over a very challenging and long course, and, wherever a rider is drawn in the competition, a clear round means that he has a good chance of winning: "The honour of achieving a clear round in the Hickstead Derby means as much to me as winning".

Ryan's King George success in 1986, when he was 17 years old, was an emotional moment, both for his rider and the packed house at the National Exhibition Centre at Birmingham. "He had jumped in the King George ten or eleven times and always been placed," recalls John. "It gets at you when a competition keeps eluding you. By then, I thought I'd never win with Ryan or any other horse."

Inevitably, on account of his advancing years, Ryan no longer possessed quite his former physical ability, but his great heart carried him to a victory which brought tears to John's eyes.

John's biggest disappointment with Milton came in the summer of 1988 when Tom and Doreen Bradley confirmed, as feared, that they would not let their horse take part in the Olympic Games at Seoul. At the time, Milton was one of the best four horses in the world. John thinks that, assuming he remains sound at the time of the 1992 Olympiad (when he will be 14 years old), Milton will not hold the same medal-winning chance as he would have had in Korea, aged 10.

1989 EUROPEAN CHAMPIONSHIPS

"Sometimes my father-in-law, Malcolm Barr, thinks that I am not aggressive enough, but every class I go in for on a made horse I try to win, and if my horse is in form, more often than not I do. If I don't, it may give the appearance that I'm not bothered, but that's a false impression. On the night before the final round of the European Championships, my father-in-law told me, 'You may be lying second, but remember that you are riding Milton and you can win. If you don't win the championship now, perhaps you'll never win a major individual title.' I think he said this to get me on my toes, but he needn't have worried. I know that championships and chances don't come around every year and I'm not as laid back as people seem to think."

Milton is now in his prime, and the first speed leg of the three-part competition well suited the combination because it was not a galloping course; there was a little bit of everything. There were three places where John managed to take a stride less than everyone else by taking advantage of Milton's outstanding qualities: namely, his big stride and the fact that he is excellent at turning back to fences.

John elucidates: "There were some quite different turn-backs. The first was to No. 3, a big oxer, the next to the water, which was a problem for some, and then straight away a turn-back to the difficult combination.

"Think about the Olympic champion, Pierre Durand's Jappeloup. He likes turn-backs, but can't take out strides as Milton can." On the first day John rode well with the utmost determination and established an early lead. "Everything I tried came off. I won, which made me feel very confident because there was no question that this was the hardest class for me. Milton did all I asked and came out with flying colours."

John had anticipated that the second and third days of the competition would be a matter of churning out clear rounds. The next test was the two-round Nations' Cup competition, which decided the team championship. "Milton felt very good. Then, in the first round he had a fence, an upright. He's not as good at these fences, but not too bad. I was perhaps a little too far off. He was not really balanced on the approach, not fully concentrating, and it all went wrong. He felt as though he was trying to put in another stride.

"In the second round, I knew we had won the team competition, but although I was now batting for myself, I still felt determined. I was concentrating hard and trying to jump clear. Then when I had the water, which is not normally one of Milton's problems, I was beginning to feel a little disappointed. After the first round I had dropped to sixth and after Day 2 I felt relieved to be second to my brother Michael."

On the third and final day, before they jumped the two-round decider, John talked to Michael: "'We have been in this position before, in 1985 at Dinard in France. You were first on Warren Point and me, second on Hopscotch.' Then I finished third and Michael ended right out of it. Michael replied, 'Well, as long as one of us wins, it will be all right, but after having been here before and blown it, it makes you think a little. Our Dinard horses weren't as experienced as these, and we were pleased to finish where we did.'

"We went in fighting, and our positions were the same after the first round. When I went in for my second round, I knew I'd get the silver medal with a clear. I wasn't considering winning – that depended on Michael. I jumped my round and was relieved to get another clear. As I came out of the ring, my first thought was that at least one of my family had won.

"As I watched Michael go I thought, I've been in the same position at St Gallen watching Pierre, when he had to have two down on Jappeloup for me to win and did not. At such a time, you stand helpless at the ringside seeing what the rider can do.

"The second round was bigger with fewer fences, but there had been few free fences in the whole competition and now the combination was very difficult and the obstacles all needed jumping. It's all too easy to have a fence down under pressure, and sometimes in such conditions it's easier not to go in last. Michael had everything to lose.

"He was very unlucky. Monsanta jumped the fence he had down too high if anything and caught the back bar coming down. Afterwards, I said to Michael, 'There's only one consolation: your chance will come. I'm 34 years old and you are five years younger than me.' But it felt very strange watching Michael. I wanted him to win, but I didn't want to lose."

Immediately afterwards, the two brothers stood proudly together, temporarily dazed, their eyes filled with tears of emotion.

Two months later, John assessed: "It felt unbelievable to win a championship after all my previous seconds: at the alternative Olympics in 1980, two European Championships and the 1989 World Cup Final".

MILTON AND CAROLINE BRADLEY

Were Caroline Bradley alive today, she would have had a chapter to herself in this book. Her sudden death in June 1983 deprived the sport of one of the world's best, hardest working and most popular lady riders. Also, Caroline lost the chance of crowning her already glowing career in partnership with Milton, who has become one of the sport's all-time greats.

In the early seventies, John Harding asked the highly respected British dealer Fergus Graham to find him some good breeding stock because he wanted to start a stud to breed competition horses. Fergus Graham sold him several mares including Pennywort, on whom his first wife, Paula, won the 1970 Foxhunter Championship; also Marius, who he bought from Holland as a four-year-old. Mr Harding owned Marius throughout his show-jumping career, during which he was

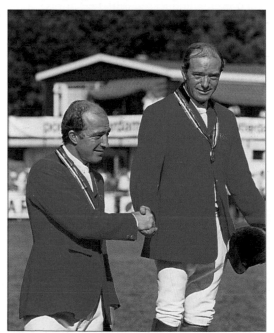

ridden by Caroline, and stood him at stud every spring.

Mr Harding used the Grahams' Any Questions, one of the first competition stallions to stand in Britain, on Pennywort, and the progeny of this union, Aston Answer, produced Milton when put to Marius. Any Questions was exported to Sweden, where he proved a very successful sire. He was ⁷⁄₈ thoroughbred and had a small amount of Arab blood in him going back to Shagya-Basa, of Henry Wynmalen fame, and Skowronek. Although Milton is of such mixed breeding, he comes from some excellent, proven blood lines and is very probably nearly half thoroughbred.

Caroline's parents, Tom and Doreen Bradley, recalled how their daughter came to own Milton. "When John Harding got down to breeding jumpers, quite typically he was aiming for the top, and either he'd forgotten or didn't want to know that there are horses in

Above: John and Milton at the European Championships, St Gallen, 1987. Despite the fact that the going was bad after heavy rainstorms, Milton's dynamic strength and John's sympathetic riding meant that they went on to take both team and individual gold medals.

Left: An emotional moment for Michael (left) and John Whitaker just after they have received the silver and gold individual medals respectively at the 1989 European Championships.

31

Above: The formative years of the future champion: Milton with the late Caroline Bradley, who was responsible for his initial training in the saddle. Milton was five years old when this picture was taken.

Right: Milton and John at the European Championships, Rotterdam, 1989: "This is a very big fence, yet he is giving it a good six inches [15 cm]".

between. Marius and Caroline had many international successes together, and his plan was to use Marius on a group of carefully selected mares."

Every year in the late summer or early autumn, Caroline used to drive over to Thame in Oxfordshire, where Mr Harding lived at the time, to decide which foals to keep and which to sell. She had always liked the stallion Any Questions' stock and, in 1978, she noticed, fancied and bought a tiny dark grey colt out of his daughter Aston Answer.

When he was 6 months old, and weaned, he arrived at her Priors Marston stables in Warwickshire and was temporarily nicknamed 'Hitler' because he was so bossy. He was also naughty and more than once managed to open his paddock gate and enjoy a gourmet stroll through the herbaceous borders.

To this day he is inclined to take a nip out of the unwary in his stable, and John Whitaker is no exception to this behaviour. When he was two years old he was sent to be broken by Bill Brown in Yorkshire, who was responsible for this phase of many of Caroline's horses' education. He proved difficult to break, and a report went home with him to Priors Marston that "He has been a very truculent chap".

As a four- and five-year-old, he was winning almost, but not quite everything, in sight. Doreen Bradley remembers that

Caroline was "absolutely furious when he did not qualify for the Foxhunter Final".

By then, everyone who had seen him in action had realized that he was something out of the ordinary; while Caroline, already a World and European team gold medallist, who was not given to lavishing praise, said quite simply, "I've got the horse of the future; he's the best I've ever had".

A wingless Pegasus, Milton, who is snowy white but technically a grey, has become a paragon of show jumping. Euphoria reigns and sports writers from all over the world flock to see him, eagerly penning features.

"Milton has become the Adonis of the show-jumping world," wrote James Mossop of the *Sunday Express*, and: "He has stolen the hearts of horse-lovers, everywhere." – this on the Sunday after the gelding out-jumped his rivals to win the Next Masters winner-take-all competition at London's Horse of the Year Show at Wembley in October 1989, for the second consecutive year, and prize money of £27,000.

In 1990, Milton excelled again when he won the Volvo World Cup at Dortmund. Then, at the World Championships in Stockholm four months later, John and Milton were in the British team that finished third behind France and West Germany. "Team-wise, we were unlucky because no-one rode badly. Milton had an unlucky fence on Day One in the speed class, and a silly one on Day Two in the Nations' Cup. It's easy to make excuses but the flashing of a battery of cameras didn't help and were the reason Milton took a fence out almost by the roots." Reaching the four-rider, four-horse jump-off made up for this somewhat, and meant that John had realized another ambition. He then had to be content with the individual silver medal behind France's Eric Navet.

Below: Milton at the water jump, Hickstead, 1987: "Milton is floating over the water. Everything is working."

MICHAEL WHITAKER

When I first knew Michael he was not as apparent at big shows as his brother, so one didn't notice him as much. But the more I watched him, the more I realized he was a rider of the same class. He is more active than John, a top-class rider who is not rough and extremely competitive on a horse – any day a winner. Michael can ride both hot and cool horses. He thinks like a horse and almost has a horse's psychology. He does not have an easy role in following an elder brother of the calibre of John.

George Morris

Such is Michael's reputation that many of his best horses, including his 1984 Olympic partner Amanda, as well as Warren Point, Red Wings, Cogshall Spot On and Tees Hanauer, were sent to him to try. Amanda and Spot were sent to be produced and sold but he kept them when he realized their above-average talent. Overall, 50 per cent of his horses come to Michael this way, and he finds the other 50 per cent round the shows and also through two continental dealers, Holland's Emile Hendrix and the Belgian François Mathy.

SELECTION

Michael finds the Lancashire–Cheshire borders an especially productive area. Jingo, and the mares Flare Path and Heliopolis, all came from this, his own backyard.

"I am not choosy about type so long as the horse jumps. If they don't jump, they are no use to me. They must jump. And I don't mind at all if they are mares, stallions or geldings. I like my horses to be very active behind when cantering and trotting – they must really work behind. But if the horse jumps exceptionally well, I'd even overlook that movement."

With the ten-month-long international season, Michael finds it difficult to take a real baby without help but can cope with four-year-olds. "At least they are very seldom spoilt, and you have to remember you don't

Far left: Intense concentration shows on Michael's face as he guides Monsanta over a jump during the 1989 European Championships in Rotterdam.

Left: Michael (left) and Veronique, on Monsanta and Flare Path respectively, put in some road work in the hills around their home.

Above: Michael on Monsanta in the stable yard at Tunstead Knoll Farm, high up in the hills of the Peak District National Park on the Derbyshire-Cheshire border.

Above right: Michael and Veronique ponder over a competition entry form. Entering the right horse in the right class is one of the essential skills for professional show jumpers.

often find any seven- or eight-year-olds without some sort of problem."

Michael reckons that even with a four-year-old, he can usually tell if the horse is going to be careful "if they touch a jump the first time and then go out of their way to clear it. But you do need the confirmation of jumping regularly at shows."

Size is not crucial but at 5ft 8in (1.7m) himself, he finds a horse over 17 hands high too big. Usually he buys horses about seven years old, "when it's done a bit and shown promise, so that after a year's work with me, it will be ready to go".

He regards speed horses as those who don't make the very top. "Hopefully, those that miss out on jumping the very biggest fences will be fast enough to win speed classes."

TRAINING

Michael has a great asset in that his Belgian-born wife Veronique, née Vastapane, is an international show jumper in her own right. Somehow, she manages not only to combine visits to support her husband at overseas shows with schooling his horses as necessary when he is away, but also finds time to compete herself.

With his abundant natural flair, to a large degree Michael's training programme is played by ear, with different horses needing different kinds of work, and some more jumping than others. In his experience, German, Dutch and Belgian-bred jumpers need a great deal more groundwork and far more work at home than, for example, Spot or Amanda.

At home he very rarely goes down to a normal free-standing straightforward fence set on its own, but rather progresses down a grid of small poles and fences to a major jump, because "This is far more interesting for us both and helps to get the horse's brain tuned in a little bit."

Fitness rates high, and he thinks that at the beginning of the season many of the jumpers are not sufficiently fit until they have been on the circuit for at least a couple of weeks or so.

The hills at Michael's isolated Tunstead Knoll Farm, 400ft (122m) high in the Peak District National Park on the Derbyshire–Cheshire border, are so steep that just being turned out for a few hours each day and keeping balanced is an automatic exercise. After just three weeks, the horses are halfway to being fully fit.

"At this stage, Amanda and Jingo pull my arms out and I move on to two weeks' walking on the roads, then two weeks' trotting and

cantering. Finally, 10–15 minutes' ground-work followed by three-quarters of an hour walking on the roads."

The local walls are of the dry stone variety and are made predominantly of the grey, stony slate that outcrops on all the surrounding crags. There are none on Michael's farm but if there were, would he jump them? "I did at my Dad's and would now if I could. It's good for the horses to have variety and jump different fences."

Nevertheless, there are three different schooling facilities: "a paddock with a fibre-sand surface, a normal paddock and a flat, 10-acre [4ha] field with a standard set of show jumps to play about with, depending what we're working on".

When the horses are resting in winter, it is far too cold to turn them out at night. They all come inside, but some degree of fitness is maintained by their being turned out during the day on the sharp inclines.

Below: Veronique scrutinizes Michael taking Tees Hanauer over a jump. "She acts as a groundsman all the time, at home and at work."

Above: Amanda helping Britain to win the team gold medals at the European Championships, St Gallen, 1987. "She's jumping very well, giving good clearance, and her front legs are together."

Training Problems

The Lancashire rider Adrian Marsh, who was instrumental in the early training of so many high-class horses, including Malcolm Pyrah's Olympic partner Towerlands Anglezarke, was responsible for Amanda's introduction to the sport.

One of Michael's major headaches has been Amanda's occasional soul-destroying aversion to water ditches. After leading the field after the first round of the 1984 Olympics at Los Angeles, Michael's hopes of landing the sport's supreme honour were dashed when the often-brilliant mare stopped in the second round, succumbing to her *bête noire*, a water ditch in the combination. Throughout her career, Amanda has remained suspect at this particular obstacle.

"When she came to me in the winter of 1981–2, she did not stop," Michael recalls. "With the advantage of hindsight, I realize that the problem was that when she was being made there were no ditches in New-comers' [Novice] classes. Now there are, but she did not see them until she was Grade A and immediately took a 100 per cent dislike to them. Even with that history and instant re-action you can get a horse to jump ditches, but they never like it."

Michael worked very hard on Amanda, schooling her over a series of specially con-structed water ditches at home. After all this she put in a dismaying stop at Douglas Bunn's Hickstead arena shortly before the 1984 Olympic Games. However, the British team manager, Ronnie Massarella, arranged with Bunn to let Michael stay on for some school-ing sessions, and Amanda ended up jumping the ditch well.

On that steamy, humid day in California in 1984 in the cauldron of the Santa Anita race-track, during the second round, Amanda was clear halfway round the course and held a fine chance of the gold medal. But ominously, the wall entry of the combination blocked off all preceding sight of the following water ditch.

"Amanda's dreaded water ditch had been differently presented in the first round. Now she did not see it until she was up in the air, causing her to freeze and stop."

At Aachen earlier that summer there had been a double of water ditches in the Nations' Cup, probably because it was an Olympic year. Amanda, who seemed to have over-come her aversion, put in a refusal. In retro-spect, Michael thinks that this probably re-kindled the problem all over again. "It was the first ditch, upsides of the lake and waterfall. The siting could not have been worse for her. There was water flying about everywhere. It caught her attention and sparked off her old problem again."

John Roberts' Warren Point may well be the best horse that Michael has ever ridden, but this high-class jumper never realized his entire potential because he was difficult to keep sound.

Michael spent the Seoul Olympics on the sidelines as reserve rider, advising Joe Turi, who was given the fourth team place with Vital, Michael Bullman's stallion. Ronnie Massarella thought the track might prove too much for Amanda.

Sir Phil Harris, a long-time friend and backer of David Broome, was in Korea to see David jump his horse, Countryman, and seeing Michael grounded, resolved there and then that he would buy Michael a world-class horse.

David's and Sir Phil's choice fell on Monsanta, an Irish-bred horse who Johnnie Greenwood, a first-class producer of horses, had bought for his daughter Gillian.

Gillian improved him, and he carried her to victory in the ladies' classic, the Queen Elizabeth II Cup at the Royal International Horse Show in 1987; but he was very powerful, pulled quite hard and usually went better for Gillian in a hackamore. He occasionally stopped in combinations where Gillian, determined but small and light, did not have

quite the physical strength to prevent him from doing so.

Michael had seen Monsanta jumping in Ireland several years previously, and wrongly thought he was no more than a speed horse. "What a misjudgment," he smiles ruefully.

He had also ridden Monsanta at the Gijon International Horse Show in Spain in the summer of 1986, when Gillian was out of action for a few days with an appendix problem. Michael had gone for three days' holiday in the sun but instead rode Monsanta three times. "I won once, was second once and fell off the other time." He had also watched Gillian jump the gelding in the final French Olympic Trial at Dinard in 1988 and remembers, "I was impressed; the course was really big and Monty jumped it easily".

The Irish-bred Monsanta, foaled in 1977, is by the stallion Hard Study out of the same mare as David Broome's Countryman, who carried him to equal fourth place in the individual competition at the Seoul Olympics. Sadly, these two horses are the mare's only offspring.

Although Monsanta stands only 16.1 hands high, his hindquarters – the powerhouse of the top jumper – are tremendously strong.

Left: John Roberts' Warren Point at Hickstead, 1986. "He always had a classic shape."

Below left: Warren Point – perhaps the best horse that Michael has ever ridden. Warren Point won two Grand Prix at Hickstead in 1986.

Michael comments, "He doesn't feel small; he has a big stride".

When Monsanta arrived at Tunstead Knoll Farm in February, 1989, Michael's major problem was that he was much bigger and stronger than Monsanta's previous rider, Gillian Greenwood, and when he first rode him, at home, "He bucked, as if to say, what is this carry on? It all feels different".

Johnnie Greenwood went to great lengths to help Michael to adjust to his new partner. To this end, he went with Michael and Monsanta to their first continental shows together: first to 's-Hertogenbosch, then to Paris and Antwerp.

His aim was to strike a happy medium whereby Michael, who is bigger and stronger than Gillian, did not use so much leg. "To start with, he had him a little too sharp and over-rode him a bit. At 's-Hertogenbosch they had a refusal because Michael was trying too hard. That was the top and bottom of it.

"As soon as they relaxed, they hit it off together like a meteor. Although Monsanta is quick and sensitive, Michael adapted very quickly and a week after their first show together in Holland they were united."

In the crucial early weeks, Johnnie helped at practice fences and with giving Monsanta the very considerable amount of work to which he was accustomed, both on the lunge and ridden, in order to fully settle him.

"He needs a lot of work or he gets fat and stuffy. The fitter he is, the more athletic he is." Michael's and Monsanta's Antwerp Grand Prix victory, less than a month after 's-Hertogenbosch, was proof that the pair had quickly come to terms with each other.

"Now I have learnt that he is very careful and that I must never jump three big classes on him in a row. For example, at the Horse of the Year Show at Wembley in 1989, after he had won the Grand Prix of Calgary (at that time the world's highest ever prize, worth approximately £90,000 to the winner) and then travelled on to compete at Bremen, I dropped him down to speed classes. He is not a horse you can hammer every day. You must drop him a level every so often."

Michael has learnt that he has to look after Monsanta very carefully, and also how to do this. He sums up enthusiastically, "When you've got confidence and he's in form, he's as good as anything jumping today".

Below: Monsanta at the 1989 European Championships, Rotterdam: "This is the Nations' Cup section of the Championships. I'm sitting a bit far forward and it looks as though Monsanta came up too soon. But we cleared the jump."

PRESSURE

Like many leading riders, Michael is uneasy when there are two regional championships scheduled to take place in a short space of time because he feels it puts immense pressure on the horses. He felt apprehensive about the proximity of the Volvo World Cup Final in Dortmund, Germany, in April, 1990, to the subsequent World Championships in Stockholm, held from 24 July to 5 August, only three months later, being concerned about the possible overstress on horses competing in both. "Major championships with three competitions, a speed and a two-round Nations' Cup type class and a two-round Grand Prix decided over four days, take a lot

of steam out of the horses. Every day counts so much, and afterwards the horses know they have been involved in a big contest; they feel pressure just as much as I do.

"I don't deny feeling pressure. Anyone who does is not telling the truth. The fact that you are there in a very good team means that you are frightened that you might let them down. It is not just the occasion, because the worry is not the same if you are riding for yourself, unless perhaps at a major competition like the European Championship, because there you are riding for Great Britain. It's not just a Grand Prix, you are a member of a team. The best riders learn how to control pressure.

"When I was in the lead for the individual European title in the final round at Rotterdam in 1989, I didn't want to get too onward bound at the big wide oxer. So I under-rode it a little, and Monsanta just touched it behind and faulted. Then he cleared the following combination, which was three from home and which had caused so much trouble, and I was runner-up to my brother, John. My one consolation was that at least the gold medal was in my family."

At the outset of the nineties, Michael, who has weathered some lean years as a result of the lack of adequate horse power, has a wealth of talent in his stables to back up Monsanta, albeit lacking in top-class jumpers with a plethora of international experience. But there is always the thought that it is better than having done too much too quickly.

The most experienced (they are already at international level), are Tees Hanauer, Flare Path, Didi and Gipfelsturmer.

Anthony Schwarz's stallion Didi, who is by the French sire Colorado out of a Belgian mare, is not only the winner of many puissance classes (having cleared 7ft 6in (2.3m) at Bercy, Paris, in 1989) but also a horse of undoubted Grand Prix ability. There is a drawback, however, because Didi is exceptionally powerful with a highly sensitive mouth, a difficult combination. Michael has found that whatever bit he tries it cuts the stallion's mouth, so he rides him in a hackamore. At outdoor venues, where there is more to distract a horse's attention, Michael finds it much more difficult to get Didi together and control him than at indoor shows, where it is "easier to keep his mind on the job".

Above: Michael (left), with John (centre) and Jos Lansink (right) – winners, respectively, of the individual silver, gold and bronze medals at the 1989 European Championships.

Left: Didi winning the King George V Gold Cup at the Royal International Horse Show, Birmingham, 1989. "Didi is giving this fence fantastic clearance. He won me 16 puissances by October, 1990, and has Grand Prix ability."

SHOW PREPARATION

The preparation of a jumper at a show, the exercise and warming up immediately prior to competition, plays a crucial part in success. Michael uses a well-tested, behind-the-scenes routine in order to get his horses into the ring ready to give their optimum performance every time.

A show like the Horse of the Year Show, which is held indoors at Wembley each October, presents problems not experienced at other shows because of its long, six-day run, its restricted exercise facilities, and the fact that many of the leading riders also have novice as well as their top international jumpers there.

The day before the show starts, Michael's box leaves the steep drive that leads down from Tunstead Knoll Farm. As well as the tack and grooming kit, head groom Janine Jones has packed a week's supply of food so there is no unsettling change of diet.

By the evening, the horses are settled in their stables (one is converted into a temporary tack room for the week), and declarations have been made for Day 1.

Right: Tees Hanauer in action at Aachen, 1988. "Hanauer is a bit loose in front here, but I like the shape of his jump."

Below: Flare Path, The Royal Highland Show, 1988. "The mare's legs couldn't be any tighter. Veronique had the ride in 1990 and was seldom out of the frame."

At the Horse of the Year Show Michael does not get up at the crack of dawn unless he has a novice qualified for the Foxhunter Final, in which case he is in the arena for the permitted half an hour at about 7.00 a.m. to accustom the horse to the glare of lights and the feel of the ring.

For six consecutive nights, Michael is in the ring until about 11.00 p.m., and often much later at continental equivalents if he makes the jump-off, so by the time he has had a meal he is never in bed before the early hours. Accordingly, if he is not up at 6.00 a.m. for a novice, he doesn't get up until at least 8.30 or 9.00 a.m.

The horses are exercised in their jumping order. It is hard to tell exactly how long this will take but the total time for four horses averages out at about four hours. The amount each horse needs varies, and also varies through the week as a horse may well need less as it tires halfway through the show.

"For example, Tees Hanauer needs more work than the mare Flare Path, and Spot [Cogshall Spot On] rarely needs more than 15 minutes' groundwork." Michael elaborates that "I can't ever be sure till I get on a horse. If he's fresh it will be more."

At Wembley, this work is carried out in the tented exercise ring with its fibresand surface or the outside sand-surfaced arena behind it. Providing the weather is decent, the rest of the time – up to three quarters of an hour – is spent walking outside round the complex. This is to maintain muscle tone and provide a breath of fresh air.

Michael usually gives a novice a jump during this first work period, but he only jumps the experienced horses then if they had a problem the previous night, to restore their confidence.

Timing in the night's major class is everything and depends on the draw. If Michael is in the first ten, he walks the horse for five to eight minutes to loosen him up. Then he progresses through a short trot to cantering, concentrating on lengthening and shortening the horse's stride, getting his complete attention and making sure he is not too strong.

If he is drawn in the first five, the horse has a few jumps before Michael walks the course. In this build-up sequence, the first jump is usually over straightforward crossed poles 18in (46cm) high in the centre. "I trot the horse over this three or four times to make him think what he is doing, then move on to a small vertical, 3ft to 3ft 6in [0.9-1.1m] high ."

Providing the jump is good, the obstacle is raised 6in (15cm) once or maybe twice, depending on how the horse is performing. The aim of these jumps is gradually to achieve and maintain accuracy.

An oxer follows, starting fairly small and progressing to about 4ft 6in (1.4m) square. If the horse is going well, four or five jumps are quite sufficient.

Michael then dismounts and goes to walk the course, while Janine slackens the girths and checks that the saddle hasn't moved backwards; if it has, she adjusts it forward. The horse has a chance to get its breath back while it is being led round so that it does not feel cold.

He always tries to watch at least two or three horses jump to see how the distances ride, then hurries back to remount. If there is a fence included that his horse finds testing, there may be another hurriedly constructed

special jump to sharpen him up. But "It's important not to overjump. So many people do, and end up leaving their jump in the collecting ring.

"If the course is big and difficult and I am drawn early, I have to be very much on the alert because the riders may retire and I might find myself called in earlier than scheduled." Ideally, Michael leaves the tent for the inside collecting ring as the preceding horse enters the main arena.

"Just before I go into the ring I usually end by jumping a fair-sized oxer two or three times, then a 4ft 8in [1.46m] or 5ft [1.5m] oxer to make sure my horse is thinking. I'll maybe put him in too close on take-off to help sharpen him up."

Above: "Mr and Mrs Raymond Fenwick's Owen Gregory, who carried me to victory in the 1980 Hickstead Derby, descending the famous bank."

DAVID BROOME

David is one of the few twentieth-century masters of horsemanship, riding and jumping, and is past the stage of being just a great rider. I have known David for over 30 years as a fellow rider and I have the utmost admiration for him as a person, rider and horseman. On the one hand he is a powerful rider, but on the other very soft and sensitive – a great combination. He has the experience round the world, not just the block. I cannot think of a country he has not shown in, and he understands courses and competitors everywhere, from the Olympic Games and World Championships through all countries, which is a priceless commodity.

George Morris

The River Severn glitters like a firmament across the seagull-spotted fields which surround Mount Ballan Manor, near Newport in Monmouthshire – as if in homage to one of the world's most gifted riders of all time, Welshman David Broome, who lives there with his wife Liz.

In continuing and typical British style, their marriage in 1976 represented the uniting of two leading British show-jumping families. Liz is the sister of Yorkshire international Graham Fletcher, who was Britain's 1988 Olympic team trainer, and who won the 1989 British National Championship with Stylo Wilkie.

David's stunning international career, spanning five decades, is highlighted by countless international successes, including two Olympic bronze medals, one World Championship and three European Championships, two of these on the late John Massarella's foot-perfect and tremendously consistent Mister Softee. David rates Mister Softee, Sunsalve, Philco and Sportsman – in no particular order – as his best-ever horses.

SELECTION

The type of show jumper that David likes best is a 7/8 blood horse. If they are 100 per cent thoroughbred like Philco, he finds they can be nervous. Since he rides a minimum 203lb (92kg) with his saddle, a 16.1 hands-high horse is the smallest he will consider. "I do not want or need a nappy [stubborn or disobedient] one and I don't like deformities. Somewhere down the line you pay the price for them."

He has found that a good horse is more often than not very generous. He searches for and enjoys a nice free mover, and "If he's any use, he'll be light off the floor. You can't hear him, no matter how hard you try. Like Pegasus and Ted Williams at Harringay when I had barely started. They made a great impression on me; the only sound you heard was the occasional pebble touching Pegasus' shoe.

"I love a horse who looks through his bridle in an interested manner with the will to win, as opposed to one who has negative wave-

Far left: David on Countryman at Hickstead, 1988: "Countryman is very tough and, when things are going right, he is lovely to ride. He has an awful lot of ability and as you can see here, he always goes well at Hickstead."

Left: David and Phoenix Park at home at Mount Ballan Manor, near Newport, Monmouthshire.

Right: Countryman coming down the permanent bank during a training session at the Wales and West Arena.

Below: The Broomes *en famille* at Mount Ballan Manor. Liz is to the left, with Richard jumping his pony in the foreground; David, on Countryman, Matthew (on Mister Cool, to David's left) and James (right, on Whizz) watch the action.

lengths and some dodges ready to try out on you." As well as hating 'nappiness', he cannot stand a horse that is heavy off the floor. "And I don't like a horse to be a hot-head – they are a pain, a continuing nightmare."

Like most experts, he has long realized that since there is seldom – or at best very rarely – the perfect horse, some degree of compromise is an essential ingredient of success. Ideally he looks for a horse that is four or five years old to bring on. He considers it hard and time-consuming to replace greenness and warns that it is all too easy to be fooled into confusing greenness with nervousness.

Concerning conformation, he does not buy a horse that is too long in the back. "I do not like an extra rib in the back. And, for me, if it is long-necked, I find I cannot control its head. If everything is working properly, you can put the head exactly where you want it every single time.

"The horse controls its head more than you – no control of the head means no control of the horse. When you can put a horse's head exactly where you want it, it's magic."

Although four or five is his ideal purchase age, which sensibly saves him a year's work before the horse has done too much, unavailability of suitable material means that David's exact requirements are not always possible to fulfil. Countryman, his 1988 Seoul Olympic partner, and Lannegan, were both six-year-olds when he bought them. Both horses were bred in Ireland, and he cites the fact that Lannegan is the only horse sired by Hail Titan to reach prominence as proof that breeding is not necessarily everything.

As far as speed classes are concerned, David does not go out and buy a horse specifically for these. "He could well last only two years in competition because of all the twisting and turning on landing, the taking it to the ultimate that is necessary to win."

He points out that in speed classes there is almost always someone with a Grand Prix or an ex-Grand Prix horse in the field. Ballywill-will was a Grand Prix horse who won David many speed classes, but he wouldn't jump water. "With him, I had scope and power to abuse." John Whitaker's San Salvador, the biggest winner in this category in the late 1980s, had the innate scope to make little of big courses.

Left: Philco clears the planks at Calgary, 1981. David considers Philco to be "one of the best big-occasion horses I have had".

"Many of the horses in speed classes are Grade As on the way down, or young Grand Prix horses being educated." He refuses to push his young Grand Prix horses. They can be two seconds behind the winner and are usually learning about handiness and how to take off and land on the turn. Money at this stage of the game is far from being a priority.

Countryman was bought from Ireland's Leonard Cave, who has given so many promising horses their initial training. He was sired by Colour Court and is out of the same mare as Michael Whitaker's Monsanta. The mare produced only two foals.

David favours a horse that "trots down to a fence and respects it. I first spotted Countryman, through a kitchen window, in mid-air over a two-foot [0.6m] jump and wasn't slow buying him. A horse must respect the pole but must also be brave, not duck-hearted. You don't want too much respect or too much courage. It's a tricky balance to get in-between on exactly the right mark."

David's ideal size is 16.2 or 16.3 hands high. Countryman stands 16.2; Lannegan is "17.0 hands high, which is too big for me. I'm a pea in a pod on that size of horse and can't hold it together easily. My ideal jumper is the horse with his hocks underneath him and a shortish stride." If a horse is built differently, David often has problems, as he does with the grey Phoenix Park, who is both long-backed and hard to shorten, whereas Sportsman and Philco could take a two-foot (0.6m) stride if so asked.

David has had consistently limited results with Phoenix Park, who is by the thoroughbred Hildenlea and not over-endowed with bone, because of an unfortunately wide variety of physical problems, headed by water on the lungs, which nearly killed him. Lannegan and Countryman are not of quite the same class and were they to be in other ownership might not be as effective internationally. With David in the saddle, there are few horses who do not perform at least a notch higher than they would for all but a handful of other riders.

David considers Lannegan to be "as kind as a Christian with a heart of gold, without an

47

evil thought in his head. He is the only horse I've had since Sunsalve who reminds me of him. It is because of the way he stands back at parallels."

Although David is continually searching for new horses, he reminisces: "Lofty [David's nickname for Lannegan] found me; I didn't find him. A man came up to me out of the blue and said, 'Would you like to find a horse to take you back to the top?' I went to see him and thought that while he had a big jump, he was not special. We all make mistakes.

"From a conformation angle, he is certainly not copybook. Although he drops away behind and disappears where most horses go up, contrary to what one would expect, he has a real powerhouse there."

He is also a natural Derby horse, who jumps new and previously unseen types of fences the first time he encounters them. He won the French Bois-le-Roi and the Irish Mill-street Derby in 1987.

The dark bay Countryman had a head start when he arrived at David's yard because "He is the same make and shape as Sportsman, who was exceptional – my all-time favourite horse. He is not as bright as Sportsman was, but he can jump and maybe has more scope. He is a lovely model with enough blood, and at 16.2 hands high is the perfect size for me. I can sit right down into him."

Having Lannegan and Countryman at the same time has not necessarily been an advantage because in early 1988 David regarded Countryman as his number one and did not concentrate on Lannegan, who was gradually returning to his best.

Countryman's chance of a 1989 European Championship place evaporated when he threw a splint on a hind leg after the Hickstead Nations' Cup meeting in early June, which necessitated a month's rest. Later, he contracted equine virus flu and stood on a stone at Millstreet. This left David with insufficient time to tune up Lannegan to his very best before the team was virtually decided although not announced.

An impressive Nations' Cup clear second round in Dublin in August was too late, but from then on Lannegan went from strength to strength. He won the Millstreet Derby Trial, the Wales and West Derby and, in October, the Norrköping and Helsinki Grand Prix.

Beyond doubt, both horse and rider had re-established confidence in each other, and in David's mind Lannegan was at least temporarily his best horse, and his performances continued to improve. He goes well on fibresand, the surface of the Stockholm arena where the 1990 World Championships were decided. Many horses do not.

David sums up, "I shall remember 1989 as the year I fell between two stools and learnt a lot". He is comforted by the fact that although Lannegan never won a prize exceeding £5,000, his total winnings for the year amounted to more than £55,000.

He also carried out some effective research into the best bit for Lannegan, who tends to get over-ambitious. "It is a case of trying to control his enthusiasm because all he wants to do is please me." After trying various pelhams, he moved to a snaffle – a broken or jointed bit – which he finds to be a worthwhile compromise because it gives Lannegan a better shape.

Lannegan's Crash

Looking back on the crash that he and Lannegan sustained at the Horse of the Year Show in October, 1987, David reckons that it was "not a fall but a disaster. It frightened the life out of him and did me no good at all. You discover that you can all too easily get carried away when producing youngsters. When they

become Grade A the temptation is to move up too fast, even if you are not actually setting out to win."

In the summer of 1987, Lannegan outjumped a large high-class field to win the Grand Prix of Franconville in France. He registered the only three clear rounds through his jumping ability and power. "He cleared every fence for fun in an encouraging experience which was entirely new and fresh for him."

Then came the daunting set-back at Wembley. "He was keen to put in a short stride three out, which left me on an unpromising long stride. If fences get bigger and, when you are jumping off against the clock, you get longer and longer, you aren't clever.

"Lannegan was as game as a cock bird and had his ears pricked. Disasters often ori-

Below: David at Hickstead, 1985: "I am just about to take off down the Derby Bank on Queensway Royale".

inate through lack of confidence between horse and rider, and these were early days. The horse mustn't have the opportunity to put his legs down in an oxer."

The combination where the problem arose was sited away from the collecting ring; there was a triple bar, with one stride to a vertical and then two to an oxer.

"It was all damned dangerous, could have hurt my horse, and you see pounds flying out of the window and his value dropping at moments like that."

Poles fell everywhere and Lannegan was quite naturally shaken after being hit by a pole on landing. "There was only one possible course – to go back to the drawing board. I never pushed Lannegan in 1988. It wasn't a year going backwards but it was a year standing still."

TRAINING

David considers that he was most fortunate to have three greatly differing but very good ponies in his early years of competition. "The first was a 13.2 who half ran away with me and could only jump off a half stride, scotching [shortening] to a fence and then jumping. He always needed an extra stride in doubles but was phenomenal and able to do 20 clears in a row. That was a wonderful early education."

The next was the famous 14.1 hands-high Ballan Nutshell, who jumped in a totally different manner, "in the old-fashioned English way, extending over the last three strides before he could jump. He was not that careful or brainy, but he looked after you."

The third schoolmaster was the bay cob Chocolate, who had one pace and jumped on rhythm. "I jumped endless rounds on these three ponies because in those days money was short – you didn't just ride for first place, but for second and third too.

"I had two saddles between the three, and consider that as a kid I was lucky to have had three such different ponies on whom to learn, because they taught me three alternative ways of approaching a fence. Every rider today has a computer for the approach – you can see who is riding by their style and don't need to be close up to identify them."

Spending his formative years on these three ponies helped give David the great asset of being able to ride and instantly adjust to a horse, rather than moulding it to himself as many riders do today. "Now that I am older, I still try to do the same, but I find that I have become narrow-minded. I no longer meet the horse halfway."

Above right: David and Lannegan competing at the Horse of the Year Show, 1988. "I would like to have seen my legs a little more forward but I'm with him. This is easy and neat. What a positive way to jump a fence."

Below: "This sequence, shot at the Royal International Horse Show in 1988, worked out well. Lannegan was in just the same form when he carried me to my fourth Show Jumper of the Year title at Wembley in 1990."

Getting the ride on Sunsalve in 1960 for the Rome Olympics was another stroke of good fortune. "It was the right time, because then I had the flair of youth."

A typically modest man, he failed to point out that one reason he is still a strong force and at the international forefront is because, despite all his successes, he remains keen to learn and seek advice.

"I love to travel the shows with my sister Liz because she's a great analyst. I remember Lannegan jumped a bad round at Hanover soon after winning the Norrköping Grand Prix. I came out of the ring in a gawking bad temper and Liz said, 'When you work him well, he goes like a good horse.' I always listen to Liz, so I got down to some serious groundwork and the next day he won like a true Christian.

"Lannegan can occasionally be very cocky and then needs downing. But, even at my age, I can miss something like this all too easily. It's worth a fortune to have two minutes of Liz's thoughts. She hits the problem on the head; it's uncanny."

Another rider David respects is his brother-in-law Ted Edgar. "If Ted will give you an hour of his time, you can't put a value on it. Up-and-coming riders should watch him in the collecting ring – I do whenever I can. So many lessons are given there and all collecting ring lessons are free. At least three quarters of the riders don't take this opportunity to watch."

He rates as "A-plus" Austria's Hugo Simon, winner of the inaugural Volvo World Cup Final at Gothenburg in 1979 and the International Show Jumping Festival (the alternative Olympics at Rotterdam in 1980), both on Gladstone; and West German Alwin Schocke-

Left: David and expert George Morris discuss a technical problem at Seoul, 1988.

möhle, winner of the Olympic individual gold medal in 1976 on Warwick Rex.

"Watch Hugo warming up and schooling a horse, especially indoors, building up to a practice jump and returning back to a walk. He maintains balance round the corners, up the straight and throughout the jump all the time until he stops. Hugo is something else.

"Alwin would jump a fantastic round against the clock and zoom into a lead which would eventually win the class. While his rivals completed their rounds and leapt out of the saddle watching the other rounds and worked out how high up they'd finish, he'd continue to work in the collecting ring to settle his horse down, concerned, perhaps, that a big time-saving stride to the last had buzzed him up. What a lesson to us all in iron self-control."

LIZ EDGAR

She is of the same class as all the rest of her family. I know her father, brother David and husband Ted, and, like all of them, she is a horseman of the highest class. Liz is a beautifully soft and smooth rider who can also be strong and effective. She has experience, having competed all over the world, and is among the handful of good women show jumpers of this century. You cannot buy or learn what Liz has; it is born into you. In her you see a sympathy and understanding of an understated, elegant nature that is impossible to teach.

George Morris

Liz is a wonderfully quiet, much respected and effective rider. She lets the jumps come to her and possesses all the qualities of her brother, David Broome. She has been a member of winning British teams world-wide, while her individual victories are legion and include two of the most prestigious Grand Prix – Aachen and New York – and the British Ladies' National Championship and Queen Elizabeth II Cup.

SELECTION

When she is considering a horse, Liz looks for one which gives a fence plenty of daylight, because "if it doesn't when it's young, it certainly won't when it's older. I also look to see if the horse is neat enough with its legs and if not, consider if I could improve it." Most of all, Liz notes the horse's attitude to jumping and tries to judge if it really wants to win the class or doesn't worry too much.

She favours buying a five-year-old because the horse cannot do much beforehand, and then it should be possible to go on and know that the horse has not been abused. She considers that four, five and six are the most important years in a horse's life.

She finds that at five years old, horses are "quite impressionable and you can get them to do things your way. By the time they are seven- or eight-year-olds, they tend to be set into other people's habits."

When buying a horse, she always likes to sit on it and jump a couple of fences, preferably built by Ted: a vertical and an oxer – a couple of poles will do and the latter need not be very big or wide. "It's not fair to ask the horse to jump a big oxer if it's young. It's the *way* it jumps I'm looking for. Rounded, neat and careful. Whatever the horse's age, it should be able to come down and jump a decent upright. If it is correctly presented and life is made easy, the ability to jump should be there at this stage."

Liz's husband, Ted Edgar, is one of Europe's top trainers, and the success of the Edgars' Everest Double Glazing Stud sponsored horses is to a considerable degree a result of his selection of likely material and the flatwork which he does. For reasons of size he cannot ride ponies, but he regularly schools

Far left: Liz Edgar and Everest Forever, Hickstead, 1986: "There's not much wrong with this. Everest Forever has plenty of height and is very neat in front."

Below: Marie Edgar with Everest Sure Thing – or 'Rodney' as he is nicknamed – in the stables. Marie prefers to do her own bandaging: she believes it very important to do it properly.

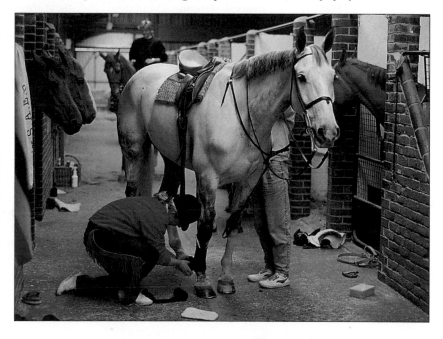

Right: Marie training Sure Thing: "It's very important for young horses to jump this kind of fence until it's second nature to them".

the Everest horses on the flat, and not just the difficult ones.

Like all the top show-jumping outfits, Ted's and Liz's Rio Grande Stables at Leek Wootton, near Kenilworth in Warwickshire, are run with a very tight discipline, and the Everest horses are noted for their high standard of turn-out.

Ted intercedes, "I'm most interested in how the horse jumps the vertical because, if it can do that, the rest will follow. I would send a novice down to 5ft 6in to 5ft 10in [1.7m to 1.8m], and if a Grade B couldn't jump 6ft [1.83m], I wouldn't want to know. I never ride anything when out looking at horses. It's up to them – Liz, Marie and Emma Mac, the ones who will be riding them – to try them."

Ted does not buy a horse for a particular rider – but because it can jump. Eventually, it ends up with the rider for whom it goes best. For example, Everest Sure Thing, who carried his daughter Marie to her unique European Junior Championship double in 1988 and 1989 and then to the European Young Riders Championship in 1990, was not originally bought specifically for her.

In addition, the rider who is trying the horse must like the feel of it. Last autumn,

Ted and Emma Mac went to try a horse in Holland. The horse impressed Ted but they left it behind after Emma had tried it because, although it had a big jump, she found it felt too small. Other than for reasons of size, if Ted finds a horse he considers good enough, he will buy it and find one of his jockeys to ride it.

Super-carefulness is Ted's priority. "When you are trying a horse, you have to remember that you can't ask a youngster to jump a great big oxer. Lumps and humps don't bother me. I've never seen a really good horse pass the vet, and if he did, I probably wouldn't want him. But I always have heart, eyes and wind checked, and the feet x-rayed."

Although Liz's all-time favourite horse, Make Do, stood only 15.3 hands high, she does not usually like a horse to be so small. Forever, who she rates the best horse she has ever had, stood 17 hands high, but she qualifies this attribute: "To be good, a big horse must ride like a small one and be handy, and vice versa".

In type, she favours a near-thoroughbred because "With the present courses, there is a need for horses to be lighter and quicker than the old-fashioned sort".

Both her two current best horses, Everest Rapier, who is German-bred, and Everest Asher, who is English-bred by Colonel Leech out of a Welsh cob mare, are on the light side with sharp responses. Sure Thing is Dutch-bred by Orthos out of Mieke, whose sire, Rigoletto, is a German-bred Hanoverian who at one time stood in Holland and is also the sire of Rapier.

"The experts class a horse such as Sure Thing as warm-blooded," said Liz, "but to me he is cold and needs zipping up. He's far better on a big occasion when there is perhaps a noisy brass band to wind him up. I think jockeys' nerves are often better on a horse with more blood when the reverse applies and the job has to be kept cool."

Marie Edgar

While Liz and Ted consolidate their respective careers, Marie (who celebrated her 20th birthday in February 1991) is rapidly establishing a name for herself in her own right.

When Marie was younger, picking suitable ponies for her proved difficult because she grew so quickly and was always a size too big for the ponies in her age group. All the time she tended to be under-ponied for her size, which gives a feeling of insecurity.

When Marie was 11 years old, she was too big for ponies of 13.2 hands high. Then when she was 12 and began to hunt on a horse, Ted realized it was the end of ponies and that Marie was very promising on a horse. Fortunately, at this time the official age for competing on horses rather than ponies was brought down from 14 to 13 years of age.

In Marie's first season with horses there was a sudden upward turn in her results because she was no longer struggling against the odds imposed on her by ponies. Riding Soft Touch, who, as his name suggests, was one of the nicest and most genuine horses possible, she reached the Grade C and B finals at the Horse of the Year Show and finished sixth. To her chagrin, both finals were won by the then Everest stable jockey Nick Skelton on Everest Halo.

Later, she was lucky to further her early competition experience on Maybe, who had been Nick's partner in the International Show-Jumping Festival at the alternative

Left: Liz with an inquisitive Everest Forever – "I think he's more interested in the mints than he is in me!"

Below: Marie with a very relaxed Minka at Ted's and Liz's Rio Grande Stables near Kenilworth, Warwickshire.

Olympics at Rotterdam in 1980. At this event (held for those countries which did not compete in the Moscow Olympics), Britain took the team silver medals.

Ted bought Sure Thing for the stable because he liked him. Geoff Luckett rode him as a novice because Marie found him stuffy and rather backward. Then Geoff finished third on him in the Foxhunter Final at Wembley in 1986. Marie had him back when Geoff left the stable in the spring of 1987.

On the other hand, Minka, who has won class after class, looked the ideal Young Riders horse. His attributes included speed and carefulness, which are the crucial elements for success in Young Riders classes. To win, Young Riders horses need to be very fast, a top Young Riders horse being an international second horse.

TRAINING

Liz could well have won an Olympic medal, and early on her ambitions lay in that direction. She is a master at bringing on and developing young horses, and that is her first love. Her priorities are simple. Many of her rivals have neither the patience nor the confidence to take time in the development of young horses.

As a five-year-old, Liz's horse, Forever, won only £300. "I didn't jump him a lot; he only saw wet weather from his box at home.

Above: Liz and the Countess of Inchcape's striking chestnut Everest Rapier make a copybook jump during the Royal International Horse Show at the NEC, Birmingham, in 1988. Rapier, whose stable name is 'The Bull', is an enigmatic horse. He possesses outstanding ability, but sometimes it is difficult to persuade him to use it.

Right: Marie and Minka, during their early days, at the Wales and West: "Minka is jumping far too high – at that stage he hadn't learnt an old horse's technique".

Far right: Liz and her brother, David Broome, discussing the technicalities of a course in Berlin.

Bad ground is no way to instil confidence into a novice. I saw that he had a very sheltered life and learnt to jump water ditches when the moment was right. By the time I turned him out in the field, he had seen a lot and accepted all I had taught him.

"As a six-year-old, he continued to progress. I asked a little more of him in the Talent Spotters' Final at Stoneleigh, which he won, and he won an international class at Dublin. As a seven-year-old he was a made horse, almost there and only lacking experience."

By the time he was eight, he was a top international. His upbringing had gone almost exactly as Liz had planned, with no setbacks. "You have to remember that even a good horse has to be lucky to have no setbacks.

"The Countess of Inchcape's Everest Rapier had a similar upbringing to Forever's but always showed an adversity to water which has stunted his progress. With him, you have the good days and the bad days. But he's made up into a very good horse."

Liz's main aim is to give her young horses good experiences, and when she arrives at a show ground, she has no qualms whatsoever about pulling her horses out and going home without even unloading them if she feels that for any reason the conditions might set them back. "Hard and smooth going is not so damaging as hard and rough. If I see hard and rough, my horses are off back home in the lorry. You can often get away with jumping a horse on hard ground once, but definitely not on Days 2 and 3. To do that makes for trouble.

"It's like a bruise on you or me. Okay, if I get a bruise, I don't risk bashing it again immediately, I take care of it. Horses' feet are the same. If you bruise a horse's feet once, nature puts it right the day after. But press on regardless, and you will have a problem.

"It's worth noting that good horses are very few and far between. Thousands of horses are registered every year but you can count on one hand those you can remember."

As far as Liz's training schedule is concerned, she makes sure that every day it is different. Variety is the key to keeping the horses keen and enthusiastic. A week's work at home usually includes days devoted to: 1) flatwork, 2) jumping loose in the school, 3) hacking around the farm, popping over hedges and shepherding the sheep, and 4) jumping down a grid.

Above: Like Liz, Marie (seen here riding Sure Thing) believes that variety is the key to keeping the horses keen and enthusiastic in training. Referring to the sheep, Marie also jokes that "flatwork is much more pleasant when you have company".

NICK SKELTON

Nick is one of my favourite riders. He gets irritated when I tease him about his knee grip, which makes his leg swing back. He gets away with this because of his great experience and talent, but I prefer the American and French leg with a classical grip below the knee, which prevents a swing. He is one of the greatest riders – positive, enthusiastic and intensely competitive. I like the way that, whether he is winning or losing, Nick is always training his horses. They always listen to him but at the same time think for themselves. He is one of the master horse trainers in the world today.

George Morris

Wen Nick was 15 years old, he had only one thought in his mind – to be a National Hunt jockey. Whenever racing was televised, he watched avidly. Then he practised on his pony, knees up round his ears, galloping round and round and round over some fences he had built in a nearby field.

The trail to show-jumping stardom began when Lol Weaver, a mutual friend of his parents and Ted and Liz Edgar, suggested to the latter that Nick went with his pony for some show-jumping help.

Only Liz was at home and when Ted returned she gave a glowing report of Nick's natural ability. "The pony is useless, but I think the lad is brilliant. He reminds me of my brother in the old days."

Consequently, Ted asked David Skelton, Nick's father, if his son would like to jump two novices for him during the first summer he left school before he went racing.

At first Nick was unenthusiastic, but his father changed his mind when he pointed out that only the top handful of National Hunt jockeys really made any money out of the

sport. Once Nick had sampled the show-jumping game, he never had any inclination to leave, although he maintains a strong interest in the National Hunt world.

Ted and Liz proved instrumental in his metamorphosis from a talented but raw teenager into a mega-star. When he left them in early 1987 to set up on his own, he was firmly established as a regular member of Britain's number one team, and he has come to be regarded by his friends and rivals alike as a selfless team man. He also enjoys the reputation of being one of the toughest competitors in the world.

His major successes include team silver and bronze medals at the 1986 and 1990 World Championships and team gold medals

Far left: Nick on St James at Hickstead, 1985: "He didn't have the best technique in the world and would hang his front legs a little – but he was very careful".

Left: Nick's early ambition – to be a National Hunt jockey – soon faded once he had sampled show jumping, and he is now firmly established as a regular member of Britain's number one team.

right jumper is seldom a bad type in terms of conformation.

He does not think that size matters, although he prefers horses 16.0 hands high, ideally 16.2 hands high. Whilst noting that Jappeloup is just fractionally under 15.3 hands high he rates him a freak, but has found that many horses under 16 hands high tend to have a rather short stride.

Despite his preferences, he says that for him no horse is too big or too small if it is good enough. His best ever horse, St James, was 16.1 hands high, and he commented of Ian Millar's dual World Cup winner, Big Ben, who stands 17.3 hands high, "He is active, but doesn't ride big".

Nick cannot countenance "a horse that looks dumb because in that case it usually is. Its face must have intelligence. I don't want to buy any humps, lumps, cuts or scars."

If he has got this far, Nick likes to see the horse ridden and put over a jump, and then he jumps it himself, assessing "if it is careful and has scope enough". If the horse lives up to his expectations and demands at this stage, he may have to decide whether to overlook the odd scar.

As far as age is concerned, he will buy a horse aged up to ten years old but "I wouldn't entertain an 11-year-old – that's too old. My ideal range is five to ten years old." He does not mind how green or young a horse is if he thinks it will eventually prove useful.

Although St James was reputed to be English-bred, Nick has never been entirely certain he was not Irish. St James, who had a continuing stream of victories all over the world, did not like to knock jumps down. "He

Top: Serenade at home. Nick sold the mare on to Martin Lucas, who she carried to a European Young Riders team gold medal in 1990.

Above: In 1990, Nick found a new sponsor, Alan Paul Hairdressing. At the Horse of the Year Show the following October, Nick and Grand Slam (shown here) won the closing Everest Grand Prix. Nick rates him "a perfect model".

Right: Nick with his speed mare, Fiorella: "She is both careful and very fast".

at the 1987 and 1989 European Championships. He set a new British High Jump record at Olympia in 1978 when he cleared 7ft 7⁵⁄₁₆in (2.3m) on the grey Everest Lastic. His big ambition is to win the World Championship.

SELECTION

Firstly, Nick looks for careful horses. Secondly, he wants to see if they have enough scope at jumping; and thirdly, that they are quiet and placid, have a good mind and do not hot up. He finds that a good horse is usually a good type. He considers that the

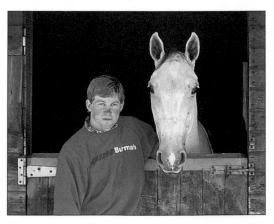

was fast with a good temperament and was an out-and-out winner and a trier with a heart like a lion. He never knew when he was beat."

Overall, he definitely prefers German horses. "You have to understand that breed. Their mentality is quite different and you must be strong with them. When you buy them, what you see is what you get. This is often not the case with Irish horses, because they are usually slow to develop.

"Germans come quicker and if they are looked after properly, they last longer. Paul Schockemöhle's triple European champion, Deister, is a prime example. When he was retired in 1989 at the age of 18, he had recently finished second in the German Championships. Liz Edgar's Everest Forever is another great example and lasted for years because no one takes such enormous care of her horses as Liz."

"I can work well with German horses because I rode so many of them in my formative years when I was based with Ted and Liz Edgar. I stress again that they are strong, but once you set about them and get their measure, they respond well.

"If you are prepared to wait until an Irish horse is 10 or 11 years old, the chances are you will have a very good one indeed." Maybe, who won Nick a European Junior Championship team silver medal in 1974 and the Leading Show Jumper of the Year title in 1978, was Irish-bred by Love and Marriage. He is Nick's all-time favourite horse because he was his first good one and he grew up with him.

None of Nick's best current horses are English-bred. His number-one string is the Dutch-bred Apollo by Erdball. The mare Serenade is Belgian-bred by African Drum,

Below: Apollo at St Gallen, 1987: "He is a very rare horse because he is so versatile and can win grand prix, puissance or speed classes".

Above: Grand Slam at the Calgary Grand Prix, 1989: "That pole cost me a lot of money. There were only three in the jump-off, and I missed it."

and most of his other horses are German-bred and bought from Paul Schockemöhle.

"I keep going back to Paul," he volunteers, "because he knows what I like. I find him very straight to deal with. Tony Elliott, who was my biggest owner, dealt with him for years, and if a purchaser has a problem with a horse he has bought from Paul, he can swap it and get another."

Time is a precious commodity in a show jumper's life, and the ability to assess a horse and not hang on to and waste time on one which is not ideally suited to him is one of Nick's assets. Picnic, who carried Steven Smith to the Leading Show Jumper of the Year title at the Horse of the Year Show at Wembley in 1989, is a horse that Nick sold on. The reason that Picnic went better for Steven was probably because he is a very powerful one-sided horse, and as Steven is a taller, heavier and stronger rider than Nick, he is better equipped physically to dominate him.

The bulk of Nick's horses are now German. Grand Slam, who has Grand Prix ability, is by Grannus and is an Oldenburg. The breed of German horses is decided by where the horses are foaled. The jet-black Top Gun, who came from Schockemöhle as a seven-year-old in late 1989 and only one week later, at the combination's first show together, won the Talent Spotters' Championship at the Stoneleigh Autumn Championships at the British Equestrian Centre, was also sired by

Grannus, but is a Hanoverian, as is the grey Governor, who is the same age. Another former Schockemöhle horse for whom Nick has high hopes is Major Wager, who is a Holstein by Landgraf.

At the beginning of 1990, Major Wager and the bigger, scopier Top Gun were the two horses that Nick had lined up in his mind as Apollo's most likely eventual successors. Unfortunately, due to a complicated series of events, Top Gun was sold to Holland in 1990, as a mount for Jan Tops.

TRAINING

Nick's number-one string Apollo is very keen and strong, and likes to progress in a forward-going way. "He's not the most ideal jumper because he likes to run forward". Nick elaborates that he "jumps from pace and has to be controlled. I have to find the happy medium. Apollo likes the big occasion and if I set my mind to prepare him to be at his maximum for a big occasion, like the Hickstead Derby, a month beforehand, I can do this." In 1989, Nick was upset that he had to jump at Geesteren in Holland to prove that Apollo was going well enough to be selected for the European Championships in Rotterdam. This was because he knew he could have the horse right for Britain's European title defence. If the horse was not up to it, he would not even try.

Furthermore, Nick desperately wanted to win his third consecutive Hickstead Derby, and after Apollo contributed a clear and a four-fault round to the British team, which finished fifth at Geesteren, the gelding was turned out in the field to let him down for a week as soon as he arrived home from Holland. Then he was trained hard every day, longer than usual and with more demanding, faster work. Nick used plenty of dressage work on the flat to help make him wait, get bunched and shortened up, because he had got a bit long, sprawly and spread out. Although Apollo likes to jump from pace, Nick has found that he must keep him short and together to be at his most effective.

The day before he left to travel to Hickstead, Nick jumped Apollo over some short doubles and doubles of oxers (wide oxers) to shorten him.

Left: Top Gun, a star of the future? "Regrettably, he had to be sold, through no fault of mine." He is now ridden by Holland's Jan Tops.

Below: "I'm working Major Wager at home and he is doing a good half pass."

At Hickstead, Apollo jumped a lovely clear round in the Derby trial, but then he tipped up in the collecting ring because he picked up too soon in front at a practice oxer. He was immediately lame.

When Nick got Apollo back to the stables he was really worried, and the following day, Saturday, was a day of 'hanging on in', fervently hoping that the gelding would recover quickly. On Sunday morning Apollo was sound again, but Nick puts his feelings into perspective: "I was a little scared that he would not remain sound as I put him over some jumps in the collecting ring. I kept the jumps low. Nothing over 3ft 6in (1.1m).

"Joe Turi went in and was clear on Kruger, and I followed. As I rode in, I knew Apollo would go clear. You get a feeling about horses when you live so close to them all the time, and that afternoon I was never more certain in my mind that if Apollo had a good stride at the Devil's Dyke he would go clear, which he did." Philip Heffer and his Falsterbo Derby winner, Viewpoint, achieved the only other clear round.

"Joe was first to go in the jump-off, went very fast but had a stop at the Devil's Dyke and a knock-down. I followed. The Derby jump-off time is quite tight, and it is not possible to go really fast at this stage of the competition because a horse can't jump at a gallop so soon after completing the demanding three-minute track shortly beforehand. I tried

Above: Apollo coming off the bank at Hickstead, where he won the Silk Cut Derby in 1988 and 1989. "He always does well at Hickstead because he's at his best on spacious, open show grounds, where his big stride means he covers so much ground."

Right: Nick schooling Major Wager: "His technique is first class".

to ride at a controlled pace with a good strong canter in rhythm and go clear. My only worry was that I was a little close, and Apollo stroked off a rail at the last. Philip Heffer then misfired twice – which meant that I had achieved my target. Apollo had won his second consecutive Hickstead Derby and the £25,000 first prize."

Some riders are unable to make the decision to retire their horses, but not Nick. In 1989 Apollo was 14 years old, and Nick decided not to use him as his number one horse from 1990 onwards. He planned only to jump Apollo in selected individual competitions with a third Hickstead Derby win for the horse very much in his sights.

Linda Jones' Apollo's splendid record is testimony not only to the bay's exceptional scope but also to Nick's understanding and training:

1984 New York Grand Prix
1985 Toronto World Cup Grand Prix
    Dublin Grand Prix
    Hickstead Grand Prix
    New York Puissance (cleared 7ft 5in (2.3m) to win)
    World Cup Qualifier, New York
1986 World Championships, Aachen
    Individual: **3rd**
    Team: **2nd**
1987 Aachen Grand Prix
    European Championships, St Gallen
    Individual: **3rd**
    Team: **1st**
    Barcelona Grand Prix
    Jerez Derby
1988 Dublin Grand Prix
    Aachen Grand Prix
    Hickstead Derby
1989 Hickstead Derby
    European Championships, Rotterdam
    Individual: **18th**
    Team: **1st**
1990 Arab Emirates Grand Prix, Hickstead

The mare Serenade had a reputation for being an extremely difficult ride when she arrived at Nick's yard from Paul Schockemöhle in August 1988. Acknowledged as possessing Grand Prix ability, a tricky mouth had denied her previous riders consistent results,

among them Britain's Olympic team silver medallist Tim Grubb and U.S. Olympic team gold medallist Leslie Burr Lenehan. Indeed, Leslie once said of Serenade, "If she can figure a way to lose a class, she will".

Nick had seen Serenade jump but never tried her until she arrived. He knew that she had always had spring and was careful but was hard to control because she likes to run off forward and had no mouth.

Nick's method of solving the problem was to go forward with Serenade, and he soon found that when faced with a half stride, she missed it out and couldn't shorten. He thinks that some of her past riders did not really master her and were scared, which gave her an advantage over them.

At first he found she was always either behind the bridle or in front of it, but never cantering nicely along. So he rode her in a normal twisted snaffle, and in his initial training he concentrated on keeping her at a walk and pushed her on to the bit, squeezing her forward with leg pressure. Throughout this stage he used draw reins, and when she accepted the bit at a walk, he progressed to a trot and then a canter.

"It took me 12 months to beat her, and to get her to take the bit. I gradually got her jumping willingly, and at first I never tried to win or go against the clock or she'd have shot off. I waited until she didn't try to grab the bridle and go."

Nick still had the occasional hiccup with Serenade because "Her former ways were still always in her mind. I had to be very aware all the time and keep in front of her movement." Nick's re-training proved very successful – in 1989 the mare either won or was placed at every show at which she competed, usually the former.

Nick has no problems with his other horses. He rates Grand Slam, who was out of action for most of 1987 with an upward- and inward-growing verruca in a front hoof (which was cut out to the coronet band), as easy, and likewise Major Wager. "I only have to work him to get him loose and free. Jumping is no problem; he's a great natural stylist, careful beyond belief, a lovely horse."

PAUL SCHOCKEMÖHLE

Paul is one of the most outstanding horsemen of his age, a combination of the old-fashioned and the modern – common-sense old and modern technical. He achieved these qualities by being taught by successive generations. You can only beat the old and the new by combining horse experience and science. It is the way Paul's mind works that is incredible; all his bases are covered and he is a complete workaholic. His elder brother, Alwin, was originally my friend when Paul was the underdog, not the star. He has scratched, clawed and worked for everything he has attained, taught himself to ride and adopted a system of riding that works for him. Whatever he undertakes, he wants to be the best. He is not afraid to work or get his hands dirty; there is no mystique about it, but an enormous amount of dedication.

George Morris

In the summer of 1988, while France, Canada and Great Britain wondered which of them would snatch the Olympic team gold medals from the United States at Seoul, a not-so-sleepy dragon in the shape of mastermind, multi-millionaire businessman and horse breeder, the former triple European Champion Paul Schockemöhle, was planning an audacious campaign to bring the gold medals back to Germany for the first time since 1972.

If Paul's strategy was to be successful, it would be an astonishing home team. For all four riders would come from Paul's Mühlen yard and would include himself and Deister.

Paul's plan was to get Deister to the top at the German Championships, where each year the results are the deciding factor in a series of competitions designated as qualifiers for the team for the major international championships of the year.

The plan nearly worked, but two fences out on the final round, when he was in the lead and selection certain, Deister twisted his back and trapped a nerve, and Paul withdrew him. "Deister was trying too hard and was very quickly sound again. The Federation still wanted me to go, but I was not prepared to take the risk so soon with my old friend; he is far too special to me.

"It would have been quite interesting to have had all the team from one stable," he reminisces in a masterly understatement.

Strangely, the situation was to be re-enacted in reverse in 1989. Then, Paul and Deister finished second in the German Championships to his number one rider Franke Sloothaak, and were selected for the team, but were forced to retire because Paul was experiencing severe headaches after riding in the unusually hot summer following a fall the preceding January.

Germany had weathered an undistinguished summer in the 1988 Gucci Nations' Cup series without one win; and, as likely Olympic horses, such as Doctor Michael Ruping's grey stallion Silbersee, went lame, their prospects seemed to be collapsing like a pack of cards.

Far left: Paul and Deister at Dinard, 1985. "Deister is the best competitor I ever rode, or ever will ride. He loves the sport, loves to compete and to fight. Lots of times when we had a fence down, it was because he was too ambitious."

Below: Paul's office at Mühlen. Over the past two decades, Paul has built up a complex of different businesses, including the world's biggest private show-jumping breeding enterprise. He spends much time each day talking to friends and clients all over the world.

Right: The maestro at home with his all-time favourite, Deister; the duo were European Champions a record three consecutive times: at Munich (1981); at Hickstead (1983); and at Dinard (1985). Paul and his riders – Franke Sloothaak, Otto Becker and Evelyne Blaton – are now being sponsored by Optiebeurs until after the Olympic Games in 1992.

Below: A group of Paul's young stock turned out together for a stretch and breath of fresh air in one of the paddocks at Mühlen.

The indomitable Paul, however, is at his best when rising to a challenge, devising and carrying out a surprise coup. He cast aside his bitter disappointment over Deister and at Mühlen, during the quarantine period prior to the Games, set about welding together a team with a serious chance of success, together with his co-mastermind, the joint team trainer, Herbert Meyer.

His riders were Franke Sloothaak, Dirk Hafemeister and Ludger Beerbaum, who were all based at Mühlen at the time. The others were Wolfgang Brinkmann and Karsten Huck on Nepomuk, who was to put the icing on the German cake by securing the bronze medal.

Considering Paul's experience, background and brain, his three able stable jockeys and the four horses of Olympic calibre at his disposal in the shape of Walzerkönig, Orchidee, The Freak and Landlord, it is easy for people to say with the advantage of hindsight that his hopes of success were not unfounded. But at the time, the British team manager, Ronnie Massarella, was one of the few who sounded a warning bell: "Never overlook the Germans. Perhaps they don't look as strong as usual, but they are always very dangerous."

PORTRAIT

Paul's three riders come from totally different backgrounds, and, although he has had more influence on show jumping in the past decade than any other European rider and owner, as a lanky 17-year-old in 1962 the West German was an improbable candidate for international stardom. Now he owns the world's biggest show-jumping breeding enterprise, and his stables certainly house over 600 horses, some say nearer 1,000. But it was not always so. There was no gilded future in prospect for Paul, the youngest of the three Schockemöhle brothers, when his father died in the early sixties; to the contrary, he found himself with nothing.

He had been riding a little for a year and knew he liked horses and working with them; however, his immediate priority was to make himself some money.

He arranged to lease some land from his eldest brother Alwin, and it is typical of the man that he immediately set to and built two chicken houses, brick by brick, with his own hands. It is also typical of his determination and business flair that by the time he was 21 he was Germany's biggest chicken farmer, owning in excess of 2.5 million birds.

While he was building up his chicken business, he made some time to ride in the evenings on horses kept on Alwin's farm. He was never taught by his brother, who won the individual Olympic gold medal at Montreal in 1976, but says that, nevertheless, he learnt a lot from Alwin simply by watching him.

In 1968 he began competing seriously, backed by his own steady cash flow, and converted the chicken houses at Mühlen into an administrative section and the first horse boxes. A year later there was a welcome turn of fortune with the acquisition of the very talented Askan.

Now, some 22 years on, he is the sole commander of his unique horse breeding enterprise, which he has built from scratch to its current estimable position. With typical German thoroughness, no stone has been left unturned in its development, and in outlook he is the complete professional.

He is also essentially modest: "I am a horse dealer," he says, but surely one on a grand scale. In just one year, 1986, he sold some 400 horses, and those that have passed through his hands have won over 100 Grand Prix. To name a few: the 1986 Volvo World Cup winner, McLain (Leslie Burr Lenehan), the 1986 World Champion, Mr T (Gail Greenough), and the 1986 World Championships team gold medallist, The Natural (Katherine Burdsall).

Many of his 150 mares are suitably stabled in the quiet peace of Calveslager, some ten miles from Mühlen where there are 125 acres and 105 boxes. The annual crop of foals is approximately 120, and the mares foal all the year round.

Masterminding the hub of his empire, the Stud Vechta, is not only his work but his consuming and driving passion. Ask him about holidays and he replies, "I had one once, it lasted three days". Vechta could be mistaken from outside for a modern factory with 40–50 assorted cars and trucks outside in the parking area. The manager of this vast domain, with its riding schools, horse walkers and two resident blacksmiths who are constantly at work, is Ernst Hofschroer. There are also six

Left: Warming up between jumps in one of the indoor schools at Mühlen.

stallions who represent the best of European show-jumping blood and include the 10-year-old Holstein Latus, a son of Landgraf I, who is considered by many experts to be the best German show-jumping sire; also Latus' beautifully moving son, the 4-year-old Oldenburg Lauriston.

The adjoining two-wing veterinary block is leased to Dr Hermann Genn, and he is responsible for the resident horses as well as running an outside practice specializing in horses. There are always about 140 competition horses in work with 20 riders, and a multiplicity of young stock, wintered and fed like store bullocks in deeply strawed pens, each containing 20 or more horses.

Olympic team silver and bronze medals and three consecutive European Championships with the exceptional Deister, to say nothing of his galaxy of Grand Prix victories and winning Nations' Cup appearances, are testimony to Paul's skill in the saddle.

He initiated the first of a series of performance Sales Internationals in 1981, which grossed £1.1 million. This had escalated to £3.75 million by 1989. A new venture was the Eurocard Classic at Bremen in September 1989, put on with Ion Tiriac, the manager of the tennis star and Wimbledon champion Boris Becker. The competitors were hand picked by Paul from both sides of the Atlantic and invitations much sought after. The first winner was Greg Best on Gem Twist for the United States, and the signs are that this initial foray into promotion could well develop much further.

Simultaneously, over the past two and a half decades, while most of his rivals have concentrated full time on show jumping, he has built up a complex of different businesses which have put him into the multi-millionaire bracket. Currently these interests are a company leasing equipment to factories, a car leasing firm, chicken farms which he leases in both the United States and Europe, a transport company and a real estate company.

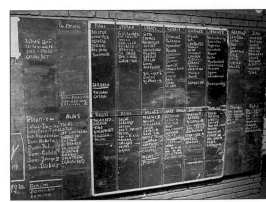

THE OLYMPIC TEAM

Paul looks back: "At the beginning of the summer of 1988, I realized we had the potential to win the Olympic team gold medals. Even without Deister I felt the same. Dirk had improved so much, as he proved by finishing fourth at Gothenburg in the World Cup final, and he had succeeded in calming Orchidee. Ludger had developed into a very cool and consistent rider, while Walzerkönig and Franke are one of the world's top combinations. All summer my target was the Olympics and not the Nations' Cup."

Paul is not only a fine judge of horses, but also of riders. He assesses the three Olympians who were all based at Mühlen throughout 1988:

Franke Sloothaak

"Franke is physically strong and a very big talent. It is not so often that such a physically strong rider has a feeling for so many different horses. Franke is different from Ludger in that Ludger programmes himself before a class and the story goes as planned, whereas Franke is intuitive. Franke can ride any horse, whether it is hot, cold, big or small. He is a very tough competitor and when he needs to be, is far more sensitive than people believe. With success his nerve has improved and he can stand pressure. He has learnt all about the management of horses, where to jump and how to prepare for a specific target."

Dirk Hafemeister

"To achieve success as Dirk has at the top level, both horse and rider must be of a high standard; and, although he has the big advantage that his father has bought him first-class horses, this is far from being the only reason he has done so well. Over the past three years he has improved beyond recognition and is now far better balanced and stiller in the saddle. Every day he rides with us and has the right mind. He wastes no chance to observe the top jockeys in action. I don't watch him all the time, but when I'm around, I'll advise him as to whether five or six strides will be best between two fences, how deep to go into a corner, what angles to make, all these details

Above: Paul and Deister, the European Championships, St Gallen, 1987. "My reins are too long. I am trying to keep contact with Deister's mouth but, because of the length of my reins, my hands are too far back. My body is about right."

Left: Franke Sloothaak, Paul's loyal friend and number one jockey, executing an accurate and powerful jump over a vertical in a qualifying round at the Seoul Olympics. Franke is riding Walzerkönig.

Above: Dirk Hafemeister and Orchidee in the main arena at the Seoul Olympics, 1988: "There weren't enough spectators for an Olympic Games – it was one of the disappointments of Seoul, not enough people or atmosphere. My hands and position are all right."

horse and must be one of Europe's best 10 riders. He made Landlord, who carried him to the German Championship in 1988, into a top horse."

Team Spirit

One of the most interesting features of the mammoth Schockemöhle horse empire is, despite its size, the feeling of tremendous team spirit, everyone working together, knowing exactly what they are doing and trying to help each other. No matter how small a problem, Paul, who is a workaholic, is on the spot when it arises, be it a matter of concern for the rider, blacksmith, groom or horse.

Franke concurs: "The key to the stable's success is that everyone from Paul downwards helps each other, everyone is important and we all work together and discuss and work out the best way with each horse. Does it need more work? Less work? What does it need? Every horse is different and has a different mentality. Everything is well organized – and everyone wants the best for everyone else at Mühlen. Paul wants us to win just as much as we want to win. We left for Seoul in a very united and determined frame of mind."

In training at Mühlen a strong team spirit was bonded. Paul rode Nepomuk every day and tried out all sorts of bits, finally selecting Deister's hackamore and bit. He also rode Orchidee most days during the three-week quarantine period.

that bring wins. Dirk is quite cool in the ring, increasingly so. He is like me, because I was not talented; I made it to the top through determination, not natural ability. If I tell Dirk something, he is already trying to organize himself and work out how to do it while I am still talking."

Ludger Beerbaum

"Ludger is a totally different person from Franke, a cold, talented competitor and an athlete who controls his body well. He is very intelligent and when something is explained to him, he can go out and do it. When he first came to Mühlen, his dressage was not good but he seized the teaching opportunities that were available and quickly improved. He is consistent, can ride very different types of

The Games

The German *équipe* stayed in a luxury hotel in Seoul itself, well away from most of their rivals, who opted for the Olympic Village. Solid and quietly confident, they attracted scant interest from other than the German press until the halfway stage of the Prix des Nations, when they were already in the lead, eight faults ahead of the defending champions, the United States

Fourteen nations took part, and at this stage the scoreboard read:

1   Germany 4.25
2   U.S.A. 12.25
3= Canada, G.B., Switzerland 16
6   Holland 16.25
7   France 18.75

The final leader scores were:
1   Germany 17.25
2   U.S.A. 20.50
3   France 27.50
4   Canada 28.75
5   Holland 32.25
6   G.B. 40.00

Germany's lead could in all probability have been bigger because Franke, who jumped a majestic clear first with Walzerkönig, did not jump again, his team having already vanquished the opposition and claimed the coveted gold medals.

The German scores were:

The Freak (Ludger Beerbaum)	0.25	4.00
Pedro (Wolfgang Brinkmann)	9.00	1.00
Orchidee (Dirk Hafemeister)	4.00	8.00
Walzerkönig (Franke Sloothaak)	0.00	–
	4.25	13.00
	Total 17.25	

These, however, do not tell the full story of the sudden drama that unfolded when Ludger's intended mount Landlord was ruled unsound, so he had to ride The Freak.

Before the first round, Paul put up a big fence for Ludger and The Freak in the collecting ring and they sailed over effortlessly. Paul explained afterwards, "I knew then that Ludger was okay. I did not have to give him confidence. It was a fantastic performance only to have a quarter time fault on a catch ride in the Olympic Games."

Schockemöhle means 'Shocking Miller', and over the years Paul has delivered many shocks to officials in connection with riders' rights and conditions in his capacity as a representative of the International Riders' Club. On this occasion, deeds proved stronger than words. With three out of the four gold-medallist riders and horses coming from Mühlen, the impossible dream had so very nearly been realized.

Since the Olympics, Paul's canny selection of riders has continued to play a great part in his ongoing success. For example, his choices of Evelyne Blaton, then Otto Becker (the latter joined his entourage in June, 1989) have been well vindicated. In 1990, the previously little-known Otto shot to fame when, among other victories, he won the highly valuable Du Maurier Grand Prix at Calgary.

Above: Paul and Deister glide over the water at Hickstead in 1986: "Deister is perfect, but I am just not straight – my legs are too far back and my body is too far forward. Deister is concentrating and confident, as usual."

Left: Ludger Beerbaum and The Freak at the Seoul Olympics, 1988: "We are safely over the third phase of the jump. After this fence I have to go left – I am looking for the turn to get the distance right to the next. Although we haven't landed yet, I am concentrating on clearing the next."

FRANKE SLOOTHAAK

Franke is obviously one of the best riders in the world today. His style is both Germanic and Dutch, a long rein and a deep seat, but he does it better than any of the others of this métier, is smoother and does not saw his horses in the mouth. I am not crazy about too Germanic a style. Franke is very powerful and smooth at the same time, a happy combination. He is big and can dominate a horse but does it in a soft way. A great competitor and definitely an Olympic rider, because no matter what pressure he is under, the adrenalin flows and moves him up. While he is great in everyday classes, I consider him better in the big ones; he's very easy going and relaxed.

George Morris

Franke is a rider of exceptional natural talent with an innate feel for horses, distance and speed. He can work them on all levels, knows how to react, and draws on three sources – good foundation teachers in Holland, then Alwin, and now Paul, Schockemöhle. The majority of riders, such as the former World Champion Gerd Wiltfang of West Germany, can ride with the utmost brilliance but not make horses. Franke has the rare distinction of being able to make, educate and take a novice to international level.

Even when he is training and competing on a youngster, he is unbelievably competitive and tries 100 per cent. Michael Whitaker is generally acknowledged to be one of the world's fastest riders, but Franke is just as fast and can produce astonishingly sharp turns. He is always in contention and, if on the right horse, the class is never won until he has crossed the finishing line.

He was born at Heerenveen in Holland in 1958, a town (until Franke's success) noted in connection with sport only for its ice stadium. Although no one in his family rode, Franke acquired a little pony, and by the time he was 11 years old was having jumping and dressage lessons on a school horse at a local riding club. When he began competing, he was immediately placed in both disciplines.

His parents could not afford to buy their son an expensive horse but in 1972, when he was 14 years old, he was given the ride on Sarno, a difficult stallion on whom he won all the qualifiers for the Dutch team for the European Junior Championships.

In the Championships (at Cork, Ireland), the team of Franke, Henk Nooren, Emile Hendrix and Rob Eras finished second, and Franke was thirteenth individually. When he was 15, Franke was the Dutch Junior Champion. Altogether he rode five times in the European Junior Championships, each time on a different horse. The horses were all sold on, and it was an early measure of Franke's talent that they all went well for their new riders.

Alwin Schockemöhle, the 1976 Olympic individual gold medallist who had been one of three experts instructing Holland's top 20 riders, was clearly impressed with the young Franke, because in April of that year he inquired through the former European Champion Johan Heins if Franke would like to go to Germany and ride for him.

Far left: Franke Sloothaak on Walzerkönig at the European Championships, Rotterdam, 1989. His style combines elements of both the German and Dutch schools and his physical strength conceals a rare sensitivity, and the ability to ride a wide variety of horses.

Below: Franke (right) and his wife Sabine riding out down a tree-lined road at Mühlen. Son Sebastian acts as the outrider on his bicycle.

Franke accepted for three months' trial each way, riding young horses. He then replaced Emile Hendrix and got his horses to ride: San Angelo and Faon Rouge, who was later jumped by Brazilian Nelson Pessoa, were two of his first partners.

In 1977, when Alwin was forced to give up competing because of recurring back trouble, he sent Rex the Robber to Herman Schridde. (Herman was at one time a leading international rider; he became a top trainer but, tragically, died in a 'plane crash in 1985.) This move did not work out. The 1978 World Champion, Gerd Wiltfang, then tried the floating grey but did not like him, so Franke had the chance.

"Rex was the dream of my childhood, the horse I always looked for." He was also Franke's first real top-class international show jumper. The pair quickly established a rapport, finishing fourth in the 1978 Hamburg Derby, then winning the 1980 Dortmund World Cup Qualifier – precursors of a string of important victories.

When Franke started riding with Alwin, he found the change from Holland hard, but "I've never regretted changing. Alwin said to me, 'If you are good enough here in Germany, you are good enough anywhere, but it would not

be so in Holland.' He was right." Franke backed up his words by becoming a naturalized German citizen in December, 1979.

Franke had already shown the talent that was to develop into an easily identifiable and effective style that has made him one of the world's most successful jumpers.

He had always been a naturally hard worker and now had the chance to learn more of the international scene and the differences between various horses. Alwin, however, had scant time to help Franke apart from some dressage work in the winter. Luckily Hans Quellen was with Alwin at the same time as Franke and gave him some help.

As all the top riders readily admit, watching masters at work is one of the best ways of learning and furthering one's education. Franke had the valuable experience of watching Alwin prepare Warwick for the Olympic Games. "I watched him train for Montreal. He was one of the best in control that I have ever seen. Very strict with himself and his horses. He worked 100 per cent and was well ahead of the others because of his groundwork.

"I realized that every country rides in the way of its own horses. One reason the German dressage is so far ahead is because the first competition horses tended to be heavy, not blood horses, and to have any chance at all of success the riders just had to learn to work their horses. Although they do not have so many now, the U.S. riders still ride in the way of thoroughbred horses. The English tend to more blood or Irish horses when they can get them, often from the hunting field. That's why they excel in the military [the Three Day Event]. The country and possibilities available make the riders. In Italy today it's different again; it's largely the moneyed ones, like that cracking horse Fiorello who was ridden by Doctor Vittorio Orlandi. Earlier the army riders, such as the d'Inzeos, were able to concentrate on their horses and take their pick of largely Irish horses, and there were many from which to make their choice, but times have changed.

"At this time, I discovered the difference between the German and Dutch mentality as regards horses. The Germans live to work, whereas the Dutch work to live. Dutch horses tend to be heavy too, but they learn fast. Usually French horses are easy; they are quick in their legs and almost always have some blood."

At the time Alwin had plenty of young horses, but many of them (such as the Grand Prix horse Alwin's Ass, who eventually went to the United States), were sold on when they had sufficient experience and came good. This was one reason, Franke explains, that "at that time I felt that I was not going forward sufficiently in my career".

The result was that Franke left Alwin amicably and set up as an individual at Damme, near Mühlen, and started on his own. Paul Schockemöhle sent him some horses; they included Farmer, who Franke was to ride for Paul at the 1984 Olympics.

The subject of Franke riding for Paul was eventually mooted, but as Franke retained a high regard for Alwin, with whom he had been for eight and a half years, it was very difficult, and demanded delicacy and tact, to move to ride for his brother, especially as the two yards are less than half a mile away from each other in Mühlen. In 1984, Franke made an extremely harrowing decision and moved officially to work for Paul.

Franke Sloothaak's 1988 Olympic partner was Walzerkönig. At the time of the Games he was nine years old, by the Hanoverian Watzmann out of a dam by Absatz.

Franke took over the ride from Bernhard Kamps in early 1988. He soon learnt that the giant chestnut gelding was at his best outside where there was more room to accommodate his raking stride, and that he was by nature excitable. At his first show, he went "near crazy in his box", and in five minutes dug and scraped a hole 1ft 6in (.5m) deep.

Now he is calmer; Franke has a different way of riding him. Inevitably he does not push or pull, it is not his style. Walzerkönig is worked twice a day, and Franke takes all the time in the world with him. At a show, Franke always puts a rope in front of his horse's box so he can see everything that is going on. Watching the others calms him. "He wants to work by nature, so that is no problem. I must make him relaxed and able to give his best."

Franke supervises Walzerkönig's feeding particularly carefully at shows because he frets all too easily and tends to lose weight. As he must not be hotted up, he has specially manufactured pellets instead of oats.

Left: Franke, at Calgary, working very hard on the athletic and able dark grey, Golan.

Below: Franke and Walzerkönig, Seoul Olympics, 1988: "This is the first phase of the jump. Walzerkönig has got a good stride in. My body is a shade too far forward, in front of him."

DIRK HAFEMEISTER

I have a tremendous respect for Dirk, who I have only known for six to eight years and watched develop from a rank amateur to an intermediate and later watched performing at the 1988 World Cup Final at Gothenburg, when he finished fourth, and the Seoul Olympics, where he helped Germany win the team gold medals. People say that if you have money as Dirk's family does, life is easier, but I do not agree. I had a comfortable background and that is one reason why I respect those such as Dirk, who have great wealth yet who fight and hustle their way up more than others with less money, even though they aren't forced to. Dirk has applied himself, worked hard and become a very good rider. He won't ever be a Homfeld or a Whitaker, but for an amateur who did not have to make riding his living he has done a remarkable job through determination, constant hard training and a continually developing knowledge of courses. I regard him as a gentleman and a great friend.

George Morris

At one time Dirk's father, Dieter, dealt in horses, and both his grandfather and his mother love horses. Dirk's first equestrian interest was *voltigieren* (vaulting on horse back). He began when he was five years old and continued for seven years, by which time he was sufficiently proficient as a rider to take part in his national age championships.

His mother wanted her son to ride. By 1969 she had prepared a nice little mare for him, and he gradually progressed through beginners' classes and a series of some more and some less suitable horses to his first international show in his native Berlin. There, in 1977, he was the tenth best overall and third in the Berliner Bear competition.

At the time, Dieter Hafemeister owned an earth moving business that specialized in road construction. He was responsible for all the work on the new Berlin Airport, and Dirk studied to go into his father's company for over two years. By now, however, Dirk's mind was set on show jumping, and in 1980 he went to Warendorf, the German National Riding Centre, for tuition. Andre Heller, who is also a Berliner and worked for Paul Schockemöhle, became a friend, and through him Dirk came to know Hans Horn, who was also at Paul's. It was through Hans that Dirk first came into contact with Paul himself. But Dirk is essentially modest: "Okay, I knew him but of course he didn't know me".

All the time Dirk was competing in minor classes, winning some and losing others "as my riding went up and down". By this time, Dieter Hafemeister had built a riding school

Far left: Dirk and Orchidee, Seoul Olympics, 1988: "I'm a bit far from the saddle here. I'm trying to help Orchidee too much with my hands and arms. She's a bit straight in her back but her front legs are excellent. Because of the pressure, I went in too deep."

Left: Most mornings, Dirk – who has moved from Berlin to Mühlen – gives Orchidee a sharp canter early on before getting down to more technical training.

Right: Dirk with The Freak (left) and Orchidee. The Freak was formerly partnered by Hugo Simon.

Below: Dirk with Orchidee, the mare his father bought from Paul, walking out of the specially built block of stables where he keeps his horses within Paul's Mühlen complex.

in Berlin with places for 125 horses, and Dirk kept his show jumpers there, making an auspicious Nations' Cup début in Plovdiv, Bulgaria, in 1985, on a horse called Borodin in what proved to be the winning team.

Dirk was now past the bottom rung of the show-jumping ladder, but still, as a non-natural horseman, faced a dauntingly steep climb. His awareness of the task ahead and his willingness to work and learn were to play a huge part in his struggle to the top. Running the riding school with his mother and jumping himself as well did not benefit the development of his horsemanship.

Dieter Hafemeister told Paul that he wanted some top-class horses for his son and help to see if he could become a better rider; so Dirk began training with Paul, Franke and Ludger for a day or so before a show and going to the shows with them.

The year that proved the turning point in Dirk's career was 1986. He was competing with Borodin and Walido at the German Championships at Berlin and reached the final round. "I'll never forget the Saturday afternoon in the Olympic Stadium at Berlin when Paul and I spoke together. He said to

me, 'It's okay to have your riding school and come for training, but you will never improve doing both, being chief of the riding school and a competitor. Both are full-time jobs; you need to be more professional. Sell the riding school, come and live at Mühlen, train with us every day and concentrate on show jumping full time. It's the only way that you will be able to improve.'"

Dirk conferred with his parents. All three agreed with Paul's proposal, and he rented the house in Mühlen where he now lives. Top-class horses, such as the grey Romantica and then the Dutch-bred Lucky Boy gelding The Freak, who was formerly ridden by Austrian Hugo Simon, and the Holstein mare Orchidee, who is by Martini and had been brought to the top by Paul, were the means of increasing international and Nations' Cup opportunities.

The Freak, who only came on the market because of a dispute between Hugo and the horse's owner, Doctor Batliner, is one of the fastest horses in the world. Dirk had to learn to sit still in the saddle and not push, otherwise The Freak would have two or three fences down. Because The Freak has so much scope he can turn very short to a big oxer or vertical. There is no big course he cannot jump, but he may well fault over a medium-sized one.

Dirk starts riding at 7 o'clock each morning, because he can sleep no longer, and works all day, training, planning and discussing his problems with Paul and Franke. This has proved a certain and direct path to improvement, increased success and – most important – consistency.

By 1988, Dirk had nothing to do with the family riding school in Berlin. The same year he achieved the morale-boosting result of finishing fourth in the World Cup Final at Gothenburg with The Freak and Orchidee. His insecurity at the time showed. When he was asked beforehand to have his photograph taken, he did not want to because "I did not think I would make the top 20". Afterwards his father said, "I see that now you have learnt to ride on a high level".

The Hafemeister horses are kept in a new, completely self-sufficient block within Paul's huge complex at Mühlen, which Paul built especially for Dirk, and it is manned by three grooms.

Above: Dirk and Orchidee, Seoul Olympics, 1988: "Here I think Orchidee is fantastic. Again, I'm a bit far from the saddle and my foot's turning out. My position is not bad but not 100 per cent okay either."

DIRK HAFEMEISTER

Far right: Paul and Dirk weighing up a course at Stockholm in 1989. Dirk has deservedly earned the respect of his adversaries because, although he does not have the innate abilities of a natural horseman, his determination and application have made him able to hold his own against the world's best.

Below: A new assurance is evident as Dirk takes Orchidee over the water at Rotterdam during the 1989 European Championships.

The move to Mühlen was to boost Dirk's upward progress. Schooling alongside Franke and Paul all day and every day, competing with them and solving problems together as they came up, meant not only a metamorphosis as regards consistency and infinitely better results, but also a new-found confidence in both his riding and approach to show jumping. When he moved to Mühlen, he was too nervous and reluctant to approach Herbert Meyer for a place in the German team, and Paul acted on his behalf; but soon he felt able to go and put his case himself. If someone had suggested two years before

Seoul that he might be a member of the German Olympic gold-medal-winning team in Korea, he would have laughed them out of court, as he was an unlikely candidate for Olympic honours but, he says, "Just before we left Mühlen for Seoul, the others all thought we were good enough to win the gold medals. I agreed with them."

When Dirk first arrived to ride full time at Mühlen, he leant heavily on Paul, but as Paul's vast enterprise grew ever larger, he spent more time working with, and being helped by, Franke. Paul had explained to Dirk that The Freak must be kept fresh mentally and not pushed or pressurized. He is usually worked twice a day, with a short morning gallop after having been gradually warmed and loosened up, and then, when he has dropped his head and become attentive, moved on to flat work.

Dirk follows the same daily training pattern with Orchidee and now understands that the key to success with the mare is to keep her collected and together. When he does not quite manage to do so, there is a danger that she will put in one of her rare stops, as she did at the European Championships at Rotterdam in 1989.

Most mornings he has schooling from dressage expert Manfred Kotter, who rides the horses as well as coaching Paul's riders on their mounts, and Dirk feels that this has helped them all and himself particularly.

Dirk would not pretend that he is a natural horseman, but with his astute brain, utter determination and unshakable commitment, he is the ideal subject for tuition. Initially Kotter altered Dirk's position, using plenty of work over trotting poles. "In former times I often had no contact with the reins to the mouth. With his help, I have learnt how to sit further back and keep contact. Not so long ago, when there was a short distance in a combination, I often had the last part down because I sat too far forward with my arms stuck out and so lost contact. I am not saying that I never do this now but, for sure, far, far less often.

"Sometimes I hear criticism that we are a factory, which is untrue. We are a team who work together. My father is keener that I should win than I am and has often said, 'I want to hear the German national anthem played only for you.'" When Dirk won the World Cup Qualifier at Dortmund on The Freak in 1989, however, he was so excited that he gave his father an emotional kiss, drowned in the exhilaration of victory as the band played the German national anthem.

Now he likes to compete at an international show every week. In the major class he does not go to win but wants to be in the top three or four places every time. But now, with the experience of riding in over 30 World Cup Qualifiers behind him, and with ever-growing confidence, he seizes a chance to win if he glimpses it.

Below: Both pictures show Dirk and Orchidee jumping the same fence at Hickstead. Of the top picture, Dirk comments: "Orchidee is not relaxed and looks a bit afraid. This is because she had just refused, and now I am pushing her hard. She is trying hard but she looks under pressure." Of the bottom picture, Dirk adds: "This time Orchidee's jump pleases me. Only my leg is wrong. On this picture it is quite clear that I feel safe. On the first, it is obvious that I did not."

LUDGER BEERBAUM

Ludger is one of the best riders on the circuit today, in the way that the same can be said of Franke Sloothaak. He is a more conservative rider than Sloothaak, and as he is also conservative as a person he is not noticed as much as a more flamboyant person would be, but this in no way diminishes his ability. He can ride any horse, from a non-goer to a hot potato.

George Morris

The German word *ehrgeizig*, meaning 'ambitious; determined', is an excellent description of Ludger. He has a burning desire to win and wants only the best results. To win top-level international show-jumping classes you must be a hard worker, which he is. In the short period he was at Mühlen, he learnt a tremendous amount. There are some successful self-taught riders on the scene, but most riders learn better and faster if given first-class training.

Ludger Beerbaum was with Paul Schockemöhle for four and a half years, arriving in January 1985 after a sound grounding with Herman Schridde. He had little top-level experience or idea of how really to work a show jumper and train him, and seized the opportunity to observe the expertise of Paul and Franke training a host of very different horses – not just one horse, but old horses, young international horses and novice horses. As well as being given the ride on already proven internationals, he was also given young horses to start, and all the time Paul discussed with him the horses' progress and any problems that came up while helping him with the work.

Paul walked the courses with Ludger whenever he could and taught him about strides down to the nearest inch. It took two to three years of constant competition for Ludger to further and improve his show experience. During this time he was also learning to train at Mühlen. He was already competitive, but that alone does not make a winner. From Paul he learnt how to get a horse to a winning standard. Ludger does not consider himself a natural talent, but he has the ability and intent to work hard. He has the vital ability to see distance.

He found the essential dressage very hard because he didn't know how to establish control and make the horse accept his leg, or "that the main object is to sit in the right position with the horse in front of me with my legs and my body not too far forward. Also that wearing the right spurs is very important." He admires John Whitaker's dressage work, which he considers nearly perfect. "I do not believe that Gammon is super-talented. He doesn't have the scope of Milton, but John has such wonderful control of him that he can win the biggest classes."

Franke and Ludger became very good friends and Ludger, who realized that his riding did not compare with Franke's, had plenty of opportunity to ride Franke's horses. "You learn from riding good horses, especially when someone who knows them well is

Far left: Ludger is a fast-learning competitor who, although he rates among the world's best, never fails to seize a chance to further his equestrian knowledge. Here he is giving Landlord every assistance over a vertical at Aachen in 1988.

Below: The Holstein gelding Landlord with Ludger at Mühlen. When Ludger was out of action for several months after a riding accident, he seized the chance to further his knowledge of all the top German show-jumping lines.

Above: Ludger, cantering out Landlord as part of his daily training routine.

Right: Ludger and The Freak in the team competition at the Seoul Olympics, 1988. Ludger compliments The Freak's performance: "Here I rate his technique as nearly perfect. Maybe I'm a bit too much in front and leaning to one side."

"When I rode The Freak, after a few jumps I felt really safe. He felt ready and jumped a big combination really easily. I rode him for just half an hour in the morning when I tried him out. Then in the evening, when the others had left, I rode him out on my own so that we could establish a communication and become friends. I did not work him and did not wear my spurs. I walked for 20 minutes, then trotted and cantered a little to learn as much as I could of his reactions in the very short time available; also I rode him in my own saddle so he could gradually get used to the feel of it."

On the day, Ludger tried not to think too much about the event and concentrated on his main objective, to clear every fence. "When I inspected the course with Paul, I knew it could work. The jumps were big but I knew the horse could jump them; a replica in our yard at home would be no problem, so it should be possible here. The reality of the fact that the horse could jump it was not changed; the only difficulty would be if I made an error."

watching. The reason Mühlen is so strong is because the riders all help each other all of the time."

Ludger recalls his parents telling him that "When I was a small boy and there was trouble, I was always very good. Pressure has never worried me." This was to prove a major asset in Seoul when his intended mount, the Holstein gelding Landlord, was ruled unsound, and Paul suggested that he rode Dirk Hafemeister's second horse, The Freak, who Dirk had very kindly offered.

"When the idea was put forward, I was not very sure or enthusiastic. I believed in the horse but did not feel myself inside. I wasn't sure if I could adapt quickly enough to face the most major test of all. Then I thought, I have trained all year to qualify for and ride in the Olympics, and I should not miss the chance now."

Inevitably, Paul had a wise and practical approach. Ludger had not ridden the horse before; to act as catch rider at the most esteemed of all equestrian contests for the most coveted prize was a mammoth proposition. Paul suggested tactfully, "Try riding him and then jump; if it's wrong, leave it alone".

Ludger was the German pathfinder, and withstanding enormous pressure left all the fences standing with a mere 0.25 time fault. This almost perfect exhibition has gone down in the annals of show jumping as one of the greatest-ever Olympic performances.

In the second round Ludger, who was determined not to have time faults, lowered the final oxer. "In the first round, I went from the triple combination to the last in seven steady strides. This time I went in six to be in time after already taking some shorter turns. The Freak knocked it down behind and I had four faults in time. It was completely my fault, not The Freak's."

Ludger considers The Freak to be the best horse he has ever ridden. "The one with the most scope; no course in the world would be too difficult for him. He is also very rideable and competitive."

Although Ludger left Mühlen in June, 1989, success has not deserted him: in 1990, riding Almox Gazelle, he was back in the team that won the world team silver medals at the World Championships held in Stockholm.

Left: Ludger and The Freak take the wavy planks at Seoul: "I rate this a very dangerous jump. The Freak is a bit unequal in front but the shape of his back is encouraging. My face shows I'm a bit scared."

Below left: Ludger and The Freak at the final fence of round two of the team competition at the Seoul Olympics: "This was the only one I had down. He is quite straight but it is easy to see that the distance I am asking him to jump is far too big."

IAN MILLAR

Ian is the whole picture, totally complete, although now an entirely different rider from the one who was already very effective in his mid-twenties at the Munich Olympics (despite his equestrian education at that time relating in some ways to that of a country bumpkin).

That we ever met was a coincidence, but in terms of his ideology he is the whole ball of wax, closer to me than any other rider I have helped. He came to me relatively late in life; this brought with it the advantage that he was mature enough to assimilate knowledge much faster than most other riders.

I consider Ian to be a forward-seat rider who rides with the motion rather than from behind, in accordance with the forward-seat school of Caprilli, Pierro d'Inzeo and Bert de Nemethy. I admire his flatwork, gymnastics and whole approach to galloping and jumping. He is disciplined and most hard-working.

He has modernized the whole of Canadian show jumping. Without his example and help, that country would not have a team of the current strength and style. He has transformed his compatriots, and I regard him as the General of Canada.

George Morris

Ian Millar has represented his country in five Olympic Games. He had won 74 Grand Prix by the end of 1989 and represented Canada nearly as many times. His long and distinguished career reached a peak with the advent of Big Ben. By any standards, 1987 proved a superlative year. He won nine Grand Prix, including the world's richest show-jumping competition, the Du Maurier International in Calgary, and, also with Big Ben, he earned the individual gold medal and led the Canadian team to victory at the Pan-

American Games at Indianapolis, U.S.A. In 1988 and 1989, the combination became the first ever to win two Volvo World Cup Finals back to back, in Gothenburg and Tampa. Affectionately nicknamed Captain Canada, on account of his results, example, and ever-continuing desire to learn and improve, he has been responsible for leading Canadian show jumping into a new era. He is always ready to help the younger generation of Canadian riders as they strive for a higher level of horsemanship.

Home for Ian, his wife Lynn, son Jonathon, 16, and daughter Amy, 14, is the Millar Brooke Farm at Perth, Ontario, near Ottawa. Perth, population 6,000, is big enough to supply the essential services and requirements of life, and the people of the town respect the privacy of Canada's most famous contemporary show jumper.

Many of the inhabitants are descendants of Scottish stonemasons, and the people form a strong, close-knit community which seeks to maintain and preserve the dignified, grey stone houses, hewn out of granite by their

Far left: Ian and Big Ben at the World Championships, Aachen, 1986. Big Ben's front legs are tightly tucked up, his muscles are taut and Ian has no need to worry as the giant chestnut treats this massive fence as if it were nothing out of the ordinary.

Below: At Old Salem, 1989, Ian (right), wife Lynn (left) and son Jonathon put the final touches to Ben before the Grand Prix. Show jumping is a family affair, and Ian is never happier – or goes better – than when his wife Lynn and children can travel with him to shows.

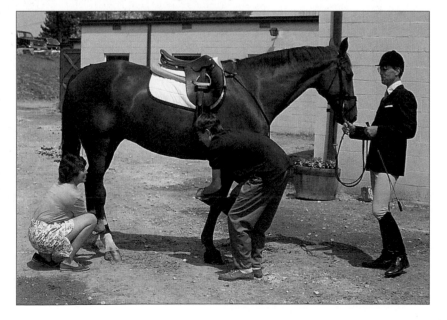

settler ancestors. Although he is away competing for many months each year, Ian is proud to be Chairman of the Fund-Raising Committee of the Perth Hospital.

The River Tay flows through the 500 acres of rolling countryside which surround Ian and Lynn's old brick house. About half the land is tillable and provides hay for the horses, housed in 25 stalls. Lynn plays a crucially important role as Ian's partner in Millar Brooke Farm.

The farm manager is Glen Bishop, who has his own horse operation at Millar Brooke. Veterinary surgeon John Atack, who competed with Ian when they were both junior riders, runs a large veterinary clinic with an operating theatre in the Millar Brooke complex. He specializes in the performance horse and standard-bred racehorses, and has many hunter–jumper clients.

Ian, who has a business degree from Algonquin College, Ottawa, first rode for the Canadian Equestrian Team in 1971, has done so ever since and has made his living from horses since 1973. Although he sells a few horses and has the occasional pupil, with his characteristically positive approach he

Above: Ian and Big Ben relaxing before the Grand Prix at Old Salem, 1989.

Right: Old Salem, 1989. Ian has walked the Grand Prix course and worked Ben in, and the two are now on their way to the arena for the competition.

decided at the outset of this period of his life to concentrate on competition rather than try to achieve a tripartite split. Prior to this he was in turn a stockbroker, radio broadcaster, real estate developer and hotel and restaurant owner and operator.

He and his friend John Revington, who he met at Algonquin, are now 50-50 partners in Jebbs Creek Investments, a company which develops commercial and residential properties in the area surrounding Perth, Smiths Falls and Arnprior. He finds this business interest, which offers the chance to do something right away from horses, a very relaxing diversion.

Ian describes the influence of his mentors using the allegory of baking a cake: "If you miss one ingredient, the end result is compromised". His first instructor was Rita Gardiner, when he was 10 years old, in Edmonton. From her he learnt that it is never the horse's fault and that it is all too easy to blame the horse and not to carry out self-analysis, without which there is not enough learning. "A rider must stay a student in order to improve; to stop learning is to run the risk of stagnation. One by-product of remaining a student is that it keeps the rider interested and challenged, questing for learning and self-improvement."

From the ages of 10 to 15, a dominant role in Ian's development was played by Doctor Otto Bode, who had dressage horses in Mrs Gardiner's stables. He gave Ian the basic skills, developing them through hours of work on the lunge line with no stirrups. "He taught me how the seat and back influence the horse's back. I learned more than I realized at the time. He also educated me in a wide range of technical skills. He was never in a hurry, and we did not work to a timetable. The horse did things when it was ready. I learnt that knowing when a horse is ready to move on to something new is important, and also knowing how to progress, and I practise these philosophies today.

"I am very fortunate to operate in an environment that I enjoy. If I were a swimmer and had to get into that vat of chemicals every day for conditioning, or run round and round a track, I can see a time when the going would get tough. In show jumping such problems don't exist for me."

Left: Ian warming up Big Ben at Old Salem prior to the Grand Prix, 1989. The chestnut is finely tuned, beautifully balanced and listening to his rider.

Above: Ian's son Jonathon helps to adjust a schooling fence for his father and Big Ben at Old Salem, 1989.

played a significant part in Ian's development by making his horses Shoeman and Beefeater available for Ian to ride. Ian, who had his first Olympic experience in 1972 when he rode Shoeman in the Canadian team that finished fourth to Germany at Munich, recalls, "Every rider needs the kind of break that Doug Cudney gave me".

Doug Cudney offered Ian the continuing ride on his horses after Munich, but with the stipulation that his horses remain at home and Ian move to Toronto. Ian considered this a marvellous opportunity but turned it down with considerable reluctance because he did not want to move again or face a regular five to six hours' drive west to get there and the same coming back east.

Ian feels that at a certain stage in his career a rider should develop his personal strategy, an awareness of the horse's need to trust and a knowledge of and trust for his horse's intent, ability, mind and body. "To achieve a brilliant performance, many elements are necessary, but initial trust is normally a key part of the deal."

Then, out of the blue, Jackie Morold of Dwyer Hill Farm phoned, saying she wanted to develop a group of show horses. At the time Randy Roy worked for her, and George Morris did some clinics for her. Ian accepted, and together they built up a string of horses. Randy Roy had worked for George Morris and knew many of George's ideas. "George loves the concept of a system. Through him I learnt a system, a structure and the organization of what I already knew, together with some very valuable new skills and ideas."

They achieved some excellent results. The horses included Countdown, who Ian rode in the Montreal Olympics in 1976, Brother Sam, Ian's mount in the 1978 World Championships at Aachen, Warrior and Bandit. Furthermore, although Ian was now the leading Canadian rider, his open mind and perpetual student philosophy continued to stand him in good stead.

SELECTION

Innate to Ian's method is the trust he places in his own instinct when it comes to seeing if a horse has the potential to make brilliant. He is wary of a horse that gives him a mechanical

In common with many of the top-level riders, Ian would be just as happy training if there were no top-class competitions. He finds the training and preparation an end in itself with the very minimum of tedium and drudgery. He compares the satisfaction and pride experienced when slowly developing the skills of a green horse until it becomes a winning international as similar to watching a child grow up.

When his family moved east, Denovan Woods in Ottawa became Ian's next mentor. "She was a good horse trainer and business-woman. From her I learnt the business end of horses; it was my first experience of this aspect. It was our shared objective to have jumpers." He also met his future wife, Lynn, who was a nurse at the time. He married her in 1969.

At that time sponsorship did not exist as it does today, and Toronto businessman and show-jumping enthusiast Doug Cudney

over water and then to immediately tighten up for a close set of verticals. For this you must have total obedience, and obedience is just as important as friendship.

"A horse has to be a natural eight out of ten in areas of talent. Maybe I can then move it to nine and a half, but if a horse is only six out of ten in the first place, the most I can achieve is probably seven and a half. The current level of show jumping is much higher and much more sophisticated than 20 years ago. A horse, to be good enough for the very top, must rate a nine in all departments.

"I'm a percentage gambler, both when buying horses and in jump-offs; I want a realistic chance of success. I would not miss a top horse because of a weakness in a certain area. When I contemplate buying a horse, I look to see what other job the horse could do if he can't do mine. In reality, the horses that will reach Grand Prix standard are very few, but they could be useful as amateur horses."

When Ian watches a horse jump, he studies its basic technique when it leaves the ground. He notes if it has its legs in the right place, draws its shoulders, picks up its feet properly, rounds its back and flips up its hind legs. He likes his horses to transfer their gallop into power on take-off because that is a major source of power.

Left: Ian and Big Ben at Calgary, 1984: "I really like this; it's the look in Ben's eye that says it all. The overall demeanour is of authority, confidence and intelligence. You get the feeling that it's part of a combination; we're looking at the next jump."

Below: "Look at Ben's hind end working; his stifles, hocks, ankles and back are pulling his hind end up. I'm moving back for balance reasons. Again my arms are straight to allow for maximum stretch; you can even see a slight loop in the reins. We are both looking in the same direction."

experience and likes a desire to please, which he regards as the cornerstone of brilliance. To him a horse shows brilliance if it transcends its apparent physical ability. Intimidation will elicit only short-term brilliance.

He considers the chemistry between horse and rider to be crucial. First, however, he develops control of the horse's mind and body and teaches it the correct flatwork. Thence, he progresses to gymnastics and jumping work while maintaining the essential element of balance.

When all this has been taught, the stage is set for the partnership to develop. Ian's horses must understand the control factor; he sees his role as that of "a benevolent dictator, but, for sure, not a democrat. However, the horses must develop their own resourcefulness, which is usually allowed by top international riders.

"So often we have to ask a horse to do something beyond his instinct – a stretch out

He favours horses that have natural balance, who are able to shorten and lengthen their stride, and horses that are aggressive and brave, although not so much that these qualities cannot be contained. "It's a fine line when trying a horse to buy. I'll try to get their temper up and then see how hard it is to make them calm, perhaps ask them to do something that they really do not want to do at all.

"Also, I like to try something new to find out how flexible they are when learning something completely fresh to them."

Carefulness has become increasingly important in the sport and therefore to Ian. His ratings out of 10 are: careful enough – 7, very careful but needs an occasional reminder – 8, super careful and rarely needs a reminder – 9–10. What he wants is a super-careful horse. "Think of the last two fences of a line being planks to a light gate, both on flat cups; there you need a super-careful horse.

"When getting acquainted with a horse, at first I try to see through the horse's eyes, then to meet him on that level. Then later he will meet me halfway, and eventually 100 per cent under my direction. For me, the art of training is to get the horse to say yes in a sympathetic manner, to use a soft sell."

Eliciting a positive response in small, inconsequential areas sets the stage for the same in major, consequential areas. "I try to set a positive mood to develop a positive attitude, but use a subtle orchestration to avoid a confrontation. Not all horses respond to this method."

Ian grew up on thoroughbreds such as Brother Sam and Warrior, who were not able to be racehorses. He found that they needed subtle handling or they hotted up, while intimidation made them frantic and blocked their learning processes. He normally chooses a blood horse that gives him the impression that it will respond; and as his career develops, he looks forward to and enjoys these horses.

He does not like those horses that need intimidation so much and prefers thoroughbreds to colder horses. "I am not a big hammer trainer. I like a horse that responds to the soft sell and subtleties. I'll repeat and repeat until I get obedience and understanding."

Right: Ian and Big Ben at Aachen, 1986. Ian comments that "we made this photo into a poster and sold thousands. Only afterwards did we discover that my left stirrup leather is twisted. I get teased about this."

His ultimate choice must be "strong under fire when the pressures of the competition are brought to bear". Because of financial restrictions, Ian usually focuses on five- or six-year-olds when buying. He goes over to the Dutch dealer Emile Hendrix once a year, has an open mind and is always prepared to evaluate the odd three- or four-year-old.

Ian bought Big Ben in 1983 when the horse was seven years old. He was over in Holland doing business with Emile Hendrix for the first time, and Emile said, "I know of a very interesting horse that you should see. Bert Romp has had him for three months."

They met at a Novotel, and the pattern of Ian's purchase differed from his usual. They drove to the stables, where Ben was standing in the aisle with a saddle on, big, slim and raw-boned. "I don't know what it was," Ian recalls of his first sight of his best-ever jumper, "I've always found him ruggedly good-looking. I thought, there is a strength and a character there. Bert rode him at a walk and then a trot round the arena. I very much liked his naturally balanced trot and the way he tracked up. Then, in less than five minutes, he was cantering and did a flying change."

When assessing a horse Ian usually lets the presenter complete the warm-up, but this time he took over at that stage. The horse's

technique over small fences was just what he wanted and, "After a very interesting 25 minutes, I was so sure that I have never bought a horse faster. It must have been instinct; the only time I have been that sure before was when I knew I wanted to marry Lynn. I didn't test Ben over mountains, just various angles, an oxer and the course that was set."

Ian's immediate problem was to figure out how to raise the money straight away. At the critical moment, an old friend and supporter of his, Eve Mainwaring, asked him if he would like a partner. They went on to form a syndicate called Canadian Show Jumpers Unlimited Inc., which has 26 members and 40 shares, of which Ian and Lynn have four. This is an investment for people with a legitimate interest in the sport. Whenever at all possible, the shareholders travel to see Ben and Ian compete.

In 1988, despite not being heavily campaigned because of the Olympic Games, Ben won $200,000, and his overall winnings are now approaching one million dollars. Foaled in 1976, he was bred in Belgium by the stallion Etretat, and Albert Voorn's mare Concern is his full sister. Ian, who weighs 170lbs (77kg) and measures 6ft 2in (1.9m), is one of the tallest riders in the game, so Ben's size (he

Above: Ian and Big Ben, the World Cup Final, Paris, 1987. "This is part of a triple combination. There are two aspects to a horse's jump – power and technique. As a result of his natural ability and instinct, Ben is a power jumper; but he is exceptional because he is also a technique jumper."

Above left and above centre: Ian and Ben in the team competition at Seoul, 1988. The centre picture was taken one-sixth of a second after the picture on the left. "In the first", Ian notes, "Ben is starting on the downside of his arc while his hind end is still being drawn up by his back. Everything alters in the second picture. We are almost at the top of the arc, and there is a roundness to Ben's back and body as he starts to go downwards."

Right: Big Ben stood up at Old Salem: power personified. He has very strong hindquarters, which are essential for show-jumping success, and an alert mind. As here, he is always intensely interested in what is going on around him.

Below right: Ian with compatriot Mario Deslauriers (left). They are surveying the Tampa, Florida arena where, in 1989, Ian became the first rider to win the Volvo World Cup back-to-back (he had won it the previous year with Big Ben at Gothenburg). Mario himself won this prestigious title in 1984.

stands 17.3 hands high) is no detriment. Ian realized that Ben had a very tough character and wondered how malleable he would be able to make him.

TRAINING

Training Ben was to prove a slow and delicate process. First, he is very aggressive, "probably as aggressive as stallions can be because of their role by nature. Normally, both mares and geldings would rather avoid problems. A horse has two options, the hard and the easy way. Aggressive horses must be trained differently or they will fight. Ben learns faster than any horse I have ever had. When the light bulb goes on, he knows."

Ben arrived in Canada after the Royal Winter Fair in Toronto in the autumn of 1983. His training began immediately, and he first competed with his new rider on the Florida Sunshine Circuit in 1984, taking part in a total of six shows.

Every day Ian encountered the same problem. He found the giant chestnut could, on occasion, be quite spooky. What was under the jumps – for example, a coloured banner – could prove disconcerting to Ben. It was a hiccup that many other leading riders have faced, and which Ian now had the experience to overcome. Accordingly, each day's schooling included much repetition.

Although Ben has a big, lopey stride, it was not as tough physically for him to learn to shorten as it is for many horses. The problem was that he did not want to learn to shorten his stride. Ian looks back: "At least I didn't have a double-barrelled problem. Size usually has a lot to do with the length of stride, but if a horse can lengthen and shorten, size is not as significant a factor."

When he went to his next show in Montreal, Ben did not have any hesitation. "Jumping is a function of experience; the horse, like the rider, must think ahead to the next fence. When something goes wrong, the mind should be in the present and the future, not the past. Gradually, the top horse will learn to stand the intensity of the course."

In the 1970s and 1980s, those with vision became involved with corporate sponsorship, and with backing from both the Bank of Montreal and Toshiba, Ian is no exception. He feels that it is his responsibility to compete in as many of the classes they sponsor, such as the Bank of Montreal Nations' Cup series and the Toshiba Classic in late July, as possible. Consequently, while he tries to give Ben a relatively light schedule, focusing on the important competitions, he makes a point of being available when his sponsors wish.

The Canadian federal government funding organization, Sport Canada, has a carding system grading show jumpers, like athletes, into A, B and C categories. Show jumpers are assessed on both individual and team results. Ian, who is in the A category, gets a monthly payment to help defer expenses.

He likens Ben's training to that of an athlete, especially now that he has learnt all the necessary techniques, and places great importance on fitness and muscle condition. One benefit Ian derives from Ben's size and strength is that big courses take less out of him than they would most smaller horses.

Additionally, there is mental sharpness and attitude to be considered. Like many show jumpers, Ben gets bored if he sits at home. "He likes seeing things and going places."

Ian is careful continually to evaluate the mental stress of competition that is imposed on a horse by taking part, for example, in a World Cup final. "The trick is to compete as little as possible in preparation; then to try and keep the trials to a minimum."

Left: Ian during the speed phase of the World Cup Final in Tampa, 1989. "This was the second last jump after a sharp right turn. As I came through the corner, I felt Ben's right front leg slip. On videos later, you can see that it had slipped to the left – he had to pick up his left leg and put it over to avoid hitting himself. He recovered from near disaster. To get over somehow, minus a rub, was a mark of a brilliant horse."

Below: Old Salem, 1989. Ian and Big Ben during the Grand Prix in this tree-shaded amphitheatre, one of the most attractive on the U.S. summer circuit.

CONRAD HOMFELD

As the Sistine Chapel in the Vatican, made by God and Michelangelo, rates among the world's greatest churches, so Conrad equates to show jumping: I can think of no other comparison. I was lucky enough to discover him in Texas when he was 12 years old and to put on the finishing touches.

When I found him in a clinic I was giving, riding a little black-and-white spotted pony, he was already a young professional, having had his mind started the right way by the late Charles and Ginny Zimmermann.

He is a freak, and I immediately guaranteed his father that, with my help, he would win the Maclay Championship and an international team place when he was old enough, which he did. From the age of 13, and until he was 19, he came and lived with me and worked in my barn.

I had the brains, knowledge and experience to take from, and was a big influence on his life. He has my ideology, both in and out of the stable and on and off the horse. He has tremendous softness, elegance and feeling, which you can't teach. It is a very rare gift from above.

George Morris

Homfeld, had "a weekend-after-work type horse, which each of us five kids rode. It all evolved from there."

He considers himself extremely lucky to have received his initial training from Mr and Mrs Zimmermann. The former had taught at Fort Riley, the U.S. Cavalry School, and gave him the correct background and the knowledge of how to ride in the classic style.

His subsequent six years, working on a consistent basis with George Morris, who became his legal guardian ("Mum and Dad signed me over."), were crucial in the moulding of an unusual talent into one of the sport's all-time greats.

Conrad describes his years with his most influential trainer: "Aside from the obvious, that he is such a fantastic teacher and very good with top-class riders and horses, who have to be tough on people around them as well as themselves in order to succeed, from George I learned that you are what you want to be and you get out of life what you put in".

This unassuming, self-critical rider is unique and has brought another dimension to the world's theatre of show jumping. A tall, handsome Texan with azure blue eyes and golden hair, he has part German ancestry but Scandinavian looks. He could well be mistaken for a movie star cast in the Robert Redford mould, but instead he is one of the globe's most highly talented show jumpers.

He combines a huge natural talent with intelligence and is quiet and subtle. Born in Houston, on 25 December, 1951, he is the eldest of a family of five. His father, Kenneth

Far left: Conrad, by now master of the difficult Abdullah who carried him to team gold and individual silver medals at the Los Angeles Olympics in 1984, clears a fence with ease at the 1986 World Championships, Aachen. Conrad again won team gold and individual silver medals on the grey stallion at Aachen.

Below: Joe Fargis (on Mill Pearl) talks to Conrad before taking the mare over some fences at home at Southampton. Conrad is responsible for much of Mill Pearl's ground work.

Right: Conrad and Joe Fargis (closest to camera, on Mill Pearl) work out their schooling plans as they ride across their palatial yard at Southampton.

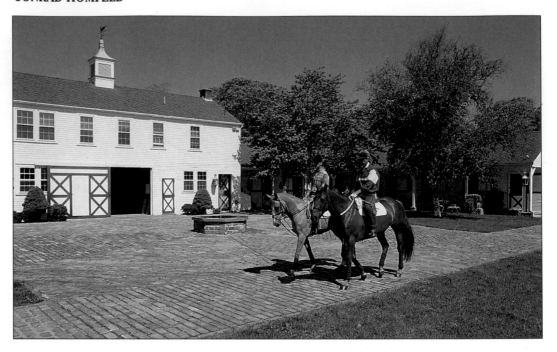

When he was 19 years old and first selected to ride for the United States Equestrian Team (U.S.E.T.), Conrad met Bert de Nemethy. "My riding style was already firmly established by then. From Bert I learned detail – he was a meticulous record-keeper – and how it is essential to build on sound principles or else everything falls apart.

"I made a rocky start with Bert, partly because we were both strong minded. It was my first team appearance, and I think we were both headstrong at the time; we had artistic differences. Now I am older I have a great respect for him."

He describes his later collaboration with Frances Rowe as invaluable, "that of horse dealer and horse trainer, not teacher and student. She could buy and sell, and I could ride. We brought different assets to our partnership. I improved during my time with Frances and also learnt the details of thorough barn organization."

The first highlights of a glittering career came when he was 15 years old and won the most prestigious U.S. Junior Equitation Championships, the American Horse Shows Association's Medal Final and the Maclay.

He won the Volvo World Cup Final in 1980 and 1985 with Balbuco and Abdullah, then, again with Abdullah, team gold and individual silver medals at the Los Angeles Olympics in 1984, and also team gold and individual silver medals at the 1986 World Championships at Aachen in Germany. He made many appearances for the U.S.E.T. but has never competed at the Pan-American Games.

He teams up with Joe Fargis in the running of their Sandon enterprise, with its 19 stalls and 30 acres (12ha), 90 miles (144km) east of New York City at Southampton on Long Island. They both have students and a flow of horses that are sent to be improved.

Some riders come to them, others they come across at shows. Among the currently successful riders Conrad helps are Louis Jacobs and George Lindemann Junior; the latter was third in the 1989 World Cup Final at Tampa, on Jupiter. Conrad's own competition riding has been at least temporarily sidelined, but he is keeping his hand in by helping Joe with his jumpers' groundwork.

SELECTION

Conrad does not have a set pattern when looking for a potential show jumper. His one major consideration is the obvious "Can it jump?", and also "the flight and feel of the jump". He is only interested in how a horse goes with the rider on its back.

He prefers to buy established animals that have done some jumping and are on their way up the ladder, ideally from seven to nine years old. "The best test for me is, when a horse comes out of the ring, does it have a ribbon on its head? Pretty is as pretty does. I like a horse with an intelligent look on its face and one that will be receptive to education; it's a hunch."

When in Conrad's and Joe's hands, the most unlikely material can be moulded into a great horse. While Conrad looks for good action, he qualifies this: "You can't pigeon-hole; take Mill Pearl [who carried Joe to a team silver medal at the Seoul Olympics in 1988]. She is a rotten mover but what a nice horse. She is also sometimes a little hot. When we first had her, she jumped inverted. She has a little stride and not too much scope. But, lo and behold, what she lacks she makes up for in carefulness and courage. She wants to do her work and always tries to do whatever you ask. This overtakes her lack of power and ability."

The former racehorse Touch of Class, who carried Joe to the individual and team gold medals at the Los Angeles Olympics in 1984, stands only 16.0 hands high. "A little peanut, yet I loved riding her. As I am somewhat tall, 6ft 1in [1.9m], a big horse is nice, but I can very easily make myself small for an outstanding tiny horse."

Regarding temperament, he feels it largely depends on for whom the horse is being bought. "Joe and I can handle a far wider range of temperament than many riders. I am always prepared to work my way through a mass of evils if the horse has the right jumping ability."

He has a very healthy respect for speed horses, particularly in Europe, and says self-effacingly that he is not good at this type of competition. He thinks that a horse's flight in the air must be quick and that an equable temperament can help out the rider. He looks for a careful horse that is quick on its feet, with an uphill rather than a downhill stride.

Carefulness he rates as essential. He considers a lot of scope to be useless if the horse is not inherently careful, especially now, at the beginning of the nineties, when the obstacles on courses are becoming increasingly light and therefore technically demanding.

Above: Conrad schooling Mill Pearl for Joe at home in Southampton. A very relaxed artist in the saddle, Conrad takes great satisfaction both in this work and in acting as groundsman for Joe. Here, Mill Pearl is totally engaged and responding well to Conrad's demands.

Left: West Palm Beach, and Conrad is up early schooling a horse for Joe. Engaging in such fine-tuning is a vital part of the preparation for competition success.

TRAINING

Part of most enduring, great show jumpers' success can be attributed to their ability to analyse their horses and explore their strengths and weaknesses, and this is one of Conrad's fortes. When the talented duo of Conrad and Joe first took over the rides on the stallion Abdullah and the mare Touch of Class, they certainly did not envisage reaching Olympic heights. The culmination of Conrad's and Joe's careers at the 1984 Olympics at Los Angeles with these two horses was "like a fairy-tale, none of it was planned or preconceived".

Abdullah came to Conrad at the beginning of 1984. The grey trakehner stallion is owned by Sue and Terry Williams, who bred and then showed him.

Debbie Schaffner had the ride immediately before Conrad and relinquished it following artistic differences with the Williams, which resulted in a parting of the ways. But Conrad lauds Debbie's efforts: "Abdullah was a stopper, a criminal, and I was fortunate that Debbie had done much of the dirty work before I had him".

At the Volvo World Cup Final at Gothenburg, Sweden, in the spring of 1984, Abdullah threw Conrad off twice. His intelligence rating was not high. In fact "He was rather stupid, and as I picked myself up from the ground in

Right: Conrad and Abdullah at Aachen, 1986: "It's a horrid habit I have, opening my mouth. I'm very aware of it – even the chin-strap didn't stop me. I tried pulling it up real tight, but it didn't work."

Below: Abdullah at the Los Angeles Olympics, 1984. "This is my favourite picture of all time; the power of Abdullah made me feel like an acrobat coming off a trampoline."

the Scandinavium, I did not for one moment think that he and I would be together at the Olympic Games that summer."

Thereafter, the treatment to counteract the refusals was to invite Abdullah to stop and, every time he did, to punish him with the stick. Occasionally he was not careful and then he was poled, which proved an effective remedy. When going sweetly he was easy to ride, as demonstrated at Aachen in the 1986 World Championships, when the other three ride-off jockeys – Gail Greenough, who won, Nick Skelton, who took the bronze behind Conrad's silver, and Pierre Durand – all got on well with him, to Conrad's disadvantage.

Conrad's problem was that although Abdullah had gone well on the Florida Sunshine Circuit, which immediately preceded the World Cup Final, his stubborn, defiant performance in Sweden could hardly have

enamoured the selectors and left them with the wrong impression. Somehow he had to prove – and he did – that Gothenburg was a one-off reversion to his previous form.

Touch of Class came into Conrad's and Joe's lives in 1979 and carried Joe to the individual and team gold medals at Los Angeles in 1984. As fate decreed, they both rode her in the interim. First she was a client's horse, then they bought her for themselves. Conrad rode Touch of Class before they bought her and resumed the ride for a time when Joe broke his leg.

In total contrast to Abdullah, Touch of Class is hot, quick and sensitive, but always a winner, even before Conrad and Joe bought her. She is a very intelligent mare: "If you send her a message, she always receives it, but as she is ultra-sensitive, she can be difficult. She is complex."

Because Touch of Class was a former racehorse, she was very lit up at the Games. The race track circling the arena and the huge grandstand at Santa Anita, where the show jumping was staged, incited memories of her former career, and the noise badly upset her.

"Touch her with your little finger and she'd react." Touch of Class and Abdullah have totally different personalities, and the key to success was to realize this and react accordingly. "If Touch of Class stopped, I would punish her but never beat her; the priority was to keep her calm and reassure her."

Balbuco was a difficult horse, both intelligent and very fearful, because, in all likelihood, he had been beaten up in Argentina, where he was bred. "He was like a frightened rabbit. If you talked loudly in the front of his stable, even that would frighten him. He was thought to be aggressive, but in fact was non-aggressive, like a shrinking violet. The key was not to think of him as the aggressor, not to send the wrong message, and for me to put the tag of aggressor on myself."

The spring of 1987 proved to be a turning point in Conrad's life. He badly broke a femur in a fall from Abdullah when competing in a Grand Prix at Tampa. A few weeks later, he was over in Paris for the Volvo World Cup Final on crutches rather than Abdullah as he had planned, helping and advising Joe.

He has now, at least temporarily, stopped top-level competition riding and divides his time between giving clinics in the United States and Germany, running his and Joe's business at Southampton, course building and helping Joe with his jumpers.

This latter activity, largely flatwork (at which Conrad excels and which he enjoys), gives Joe increased confidence and resilience. "Joe's presence on a horse is very strong, whereas it's as though I'm not there. I'm in charge of the homework, and the mix of me on the flat and Joe showing does well." Conrad enjoys riding behind the scenes, doing the preparation and getting the horses tuned up.

Many riders find themselves unable to give up competing and to reorganise and reorientate their lives within or outside the sport. Conrad assesses his feelings: "I've always had physical fear, and as you get older you feel the physical side of the sport, and my accident brought this more to the surface. The Abdullah years were very hard, and you don't have quite the same competitive feeling; you burn out.

"I'm not in awe of what I'm doing. I can live with or without competition. I'm not interested in little classes. I like the big events and going for the jugular, and then I want to be in the top three. I'll ride again and compete again, but only if the right horse turns up. I don't take half measures; that's one of my personality flaws. I like to get it right."

Below: Conrad at work in a practice arena at West Palm Beach. The bay, one of Joe's novices, has an excellent top line in this extended trot.

Above: From left to right are Katie Monahan Prudent, Mike Matz and Conrad – three of the team of four who won the team gold medals in the World Championships at Aachen in 1986 for the U.S. The three look very confident as they walk the course together.

Like all great riders, Conrad is an avid observer of his rivals. In Europe he especially likes Nelson Pessoa, David Broome and Nick Skelton. His ideal show jumper would possess the red-haired Virginian Rodney Jenkins' incredible natural gifts and triple European Champion Paul Schockemöhle's brain: "That combination would be unbeatable".

COURSE DESIGNING

Conrad has always been fascinated by course designing. "I like it more than riding; it's very solitary, just you and your imagination. You don't have to deal with the horse's mind."

He began course designing as far back as 1972, not at major events but at little national shows. It was Frances Rowe who helped him most and who eventually recommended him for his first plum job. "My course designing has not been all that public because I was wearing a rider's hat at the beginning and I could earn more extra money at the time by giving clinics.

"Now, I like to do no more than two Grand Prix a year or I'm over-used. My departure point is that of a rider. I like to play a little rough; that favours me. I like to stretch and be stretched. I know that if I am a little stretched, the others will be gasping for air. I have never liked mediocre winners. I applaud David Broome and Michael Whitaker. I want my courses to make the cream rise to the top."

When he designs for the bottom level – novices – his courses tend to be a lower-level version of the top. "I like continuity, so my training division courses are watered down versions of Grand Prix courses.

"I think it's an advantage to a course builder to have been a rider. As a rider, I like to be curious when I walk a course. I try to do this as a course builder."

When designing a Grand Prix course, he demands scope – somewhere there is always a requirement for that quality – and also carefulness, so his courses invariably include some jumps that fall easily. He likes turns and transitions in lines to test a horse's pliability.

A horse must act promptly, because his time allowance is always fairly tight. "If a horse is hanging about, he'll get time faults. A tight time allowance favours a good rider – a dunce won't manage. David Broome would find gaps in the course where he could save time. I like to favour the good riders.

"My hallmark is the inclusion of forward to tight, and tight to forward, strides. I intentionally steer away from oxer to oxer because that's black and white and I like the greys more. I love dry ditches, open water and Liverpools [jumps over a water ditch]. Water is a fair and valid test, and I like using it to keep the jumping down, placing the water so that a horse might spook and have a rail."

Conrad recalls Olaf Petersen's combination at the Volvo World Cup Final at Berlin in 1985, when he scored his second victory, this time on Abdullah, over Nick Skelton and Everest St James, Pierre Durand and Jappeloup and Malcolm Pyrah and Towerlands Anglezarke. "It was sighted away from the gate and came early on in the course. All four elements were big: a first oxer, one forward stride to another oxer, a tight two strides to a vertical, and finally, a tight stride to a vertical. It was a difficult and interesting problem. In contrast, I try to be more subtle and a little less obvious.

"As a course designer, you can't always put jumps where you want, but a course's limitations are usually in the human mind. If someone tried to stop me doing something I had planned, I'd try and be flexible, but if I thought it was unreasonable, there'd be blood on the floor that night. I try to be unstereotyped; I can't be stamped because I do so few courses. I build no meat-and-potato courses; I try to be imaginative and innovative.

"In the United States we are so backward and retarded. There are no people to paint poles or armies to move fences. What can you expect from the nation who invented McDonalds? I am fortunate to build for the week-long Southampton Show with the Hampton Grand Prix in the main ring, because the committee there gives me much more support than most U.S. shows are able to do."

Conrad, who built for the first Tampa Grand Prix in spring 1989, which was won by Louis Jacobs on Janus de Ver, would love to build an Olympic Games course when he has more international experience, and considers it "vital to remain critical of your own work and all too easy to become complacent and not do so. The biggest measuring stick is, did you get a good result and was it gotten in a humane way?"

To date, his most significant accolade has been designing for the final U.S. Olympic Selection Trials at Southampton in 1988 and the U.S.E.T. show-jumping championship, and his course-designing prowess has been recognized by the American Horse Shows Association, which gave him a special award.

He works out his courses indoors on graph paper. "They come pretty quickly; I see it all in my head. I like lines, a gymnastic line with a lot going on in it, and connected jumps, four, five or maybe six somehow related. As an example, I liked the first part of Bert de Nemethy's course for the 1989 Tampa Invitational in Tampa Stadium. I admire his work and Olaf Petersen's curves and diagonal lines, and I love Philippe Gayot's work.

"The fact that I have competed means that I can throw in what I then dreaded, but it is not a prerequisite that a course designer should have ridden. The bottom line is the horse. Can you get a good result and not injure the livestock? You must be conscientious and have some knowledge.

"I like softness, which is my vice as a rider but perhaps my virtue as a course designer. I want to get and take chances but I don't want to do ordinary work. I want to break new ground using my knowledge and experience. But while I'm not afraid to take a chance, I don't want horses hurt or riders on the floor.

"Course designing in the United States means rotten pay; you can make four times as much giving a clinic. You only course design because you love it, despite the conditions, occasional belly-aches and impossible schedules that you sometimes have to face with no crew."

Joe Fargis, who has tackled many of Conrad's courses, assesses, "If a horse is well broken, it will cope with Conrad's courses well. They are not as high as some but are more technical than most. He tries to stretch both horse and rider without demanding a large scopey effort on the part of the horse. It is not a matter of pure power. To succeed over his courses, a talented and thoroughly schooled horse is what is needed. His taste in shape and design is totally different from any other in the States."

Below: Conrad and Abdullah at Aachen, 1986: "Look at his expression – he's focusing on his work. I was lucky to be his rider, but the way he went was no accident: I had done my homework and he was fully prepared. He's doing his work and doing it happily."

JOE FARGIS

Joe is a master horseman of the old school, the old-fashioned one which I prefer. He understands horses, cares for them, and schools in a simple way with a beautifully made forward seat of the school of Mrs Dillon, Captain Littauer and Bert de Nemethy. Captain Littauer was a Russian immigrant and an advocate of the forward seat who changed ideology. Formerly in the cavalry school in the days of the last Czar in imperial Russia, he rode with a dressage seat.

Joe and I have a similarity of beginnings; we don't overjump, don't overcollect, and relate closely.

Conrad and Joe are very different. Conrad had to learn to be a tougher rider because he was basically an under-rider, whereas Joe was innately stronger and had to learn to adapt vice versa.

George Morris

Meeting him for the first time, a stranger would never guess that Joe – modest, self-effacing and self-critical – is one of the most talented show jumpers ever. Joe considers himself fortunate to have been exposed to "four of the best", who were responsible for his tuition and metamorphosis into a show-jumping mega-star. Born in New York City, he is the son of a salesman of French heritage (the family's original name was du Farge) whose wife was of Irish ancestry. Neither of them had any equestrian connections whatsoever.

From the ages of 7 to 18 Joe made a fabulous start with Jane Dillon. She taught him about love for the animal. "I had no idea that competition existed and I had a very good time. It was the perfect start for a young child. Mrs Dillon ran a happy camp in terms of both ambiance and environment. From her I learnt that the horse comes first and how to take care of him. At an early age we were taught the basics of stable management: the early signs of sickness, lameness and injuries, a general theory of things, and the practical application of the theory."

Frances Rowe, who died in 1985, taught him first and foremost about horses. Joe was with her from 1966 to 1978 and says, "She instilled into me the fact that the horse is a living, breathing creature, not a machine or vehicle for the achievement of success".

She stressed the importance of getting every single detail right – blacksmith, food, teeth, groom. "You have to remember that the horse is our captive and thus his destiny is in our hands. We control all his moves and so have a big responsibility to supervise his life. He must at all times be considered first and be treated in the best way we know, because he is doing a lot for us."

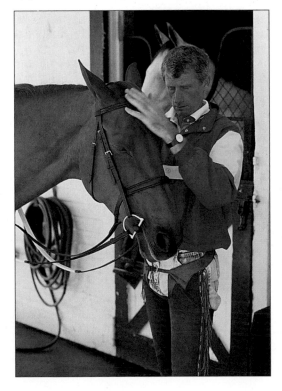

Far left: Joe Fargis and Mill Pearl helping the U.S. team to the silver medals at the Seoul Olympics, 1988.

Left: In the stables at Southampton. A pat for Mill Pearl from Joe after another hard training session.

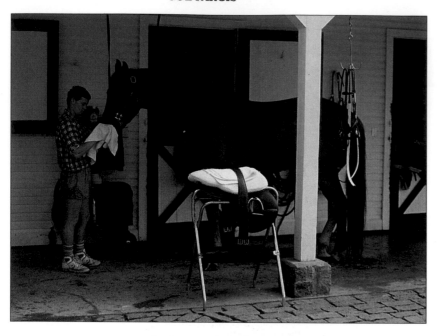

Above: A groom at work in Conrad's and Joe's barn at the Southampton stables.

"This thought should come last, and I know it sounds crazy, but I do like a horse with an intelligent face; after all, I have to look at it every day."

Joe's priorities are soundness and a very good mentality. "The latter is vital in this day and age, more important than scope; you do not want a big, powerful brute whose mentality means that he can't be trained."

As a sub-topic of mentality he stresses that a horse must want to jump clear, be careful and have a certain respect for jumps, the instinct to want to get over them without knocking them down.

He rates athletic ability highly and says that a horse "has to look attractive. Balbuco did not, but he had the redeeming quality of tremendous presence, rather like Paul Schockemöhle's Deister. Think of Jappeloup, Heidi Robbiani's 1984 Olympic individual bronze medallist, Jessica, and Melanie Smith's Calypso – their faces are perceptive. It's not an exaggeration, not a fairy-tale; intelligence shows. Milton is totally different. He has a great face; standing still, he can look just like a Shetland pony physically, but when he's in the ring galloping down to a big fence, it is a totally different story."

He considers speed classes to be a great test for any horse: "To jump fast, be clear at the same time and keep presence of mind is very demanding. If a horse is asked to do this every day, it will soon think the object is to go as fast as it can, all the time. The very nature of the class stretches the horse's mentality, and you must be careful about doing too many speed classes with a horse."

Part of Mill Pearl's training schedule consists of speed classes, but only every now and then. "When I do speed classes, the advantage is that the jumps are small and she's eager; then, when she tackles bigger Grand Prix type jumps, they cause her no problem. I use occasional speed classes as confidence builders, not for the sake of speed itself, but for the opportunity they present to face smaller courses as well."

Joe uses Mill Pearl for speed classes rather sparingly, just as Paul Schockemöhle did Deister. This is because Mill Pearl is not the most powerful horse in the world and it would discourage her if she quite unnecessarily faced giant jumps every day.

Bert de Nemethy taught Joe all his knowledge of sophisticated riding, "if such can indeed be attributed to me. He taught me dressage training and how it relates to jumping, and – most important – that there are no tricks or short cuts."

In other words, Bert taught him the classical approach, the system on which Joe's skills are founded.

"The ideal is to have control, to be in control from the very first step, developing through the walk, trot and canter. Control every movement, make the walk perfect and pay attention to every single, even minor, detail, such as cleaning your boots and cleaning your tack, and then, eventually, the big picture will fall into place."

Joe's fourth and continuing mentor is his long-time friend and business partner, Conrad Homfeld. "He's so good I can learn from just watching. When I'm riding I picture Conrad and imagine what he'd do. I've been very lucky to have been exposed to four outstanding horse masters."

SELECTION

"For me there is no ideal age; if the horse is good and I like it, I trust myself, and providing I have the means, I use my first instinct and go ahead and buy it.

Joe, who is 6ft 2in (1.9m) tall and weighs 165lb (75kg), says, "I've learnt not to disregard a horse because it's small; that's a preconceived notion. Too big a horse could be a problem because of the high degree of coordination needed over today's courses. Think of Touch of Class and Jappeloup, the winners of the last two Olympic Games. They stand 16.0 and 15.3 hands high. Melanie Smith's 1984 Olympic team gold medallist, Calypso, is also a small horse."

TRAINING

Emphasizing that the breeding of world-class show jumpers is so often a matter of chance, Joe points out that Mill Pearl could very easily not even have been conceived. In 1978, Noel C. Duggan, who owns the top Irish show-jumping complex of Millstreet in County Cork, bought a barren thoroughbred mare by Anthony for £300. "To save her from the factory, it was; I knew the remedy to get her in foal," he recalls.

The remedy proved successful. He sent the mare to the Irish draught stallion King of Diamonds, who has been responsible for so many good show jumpers, and in the following year, 1979, Mill Pearl was foaled.

Joe bought Mill Pearl, who is now owned by Mr and Mrs Patrick Butler and Jane Burr, in 1985, when she was a six-year-old. At first she was just jumped along with all the others of her age and experience. It was by no means a production like preparing Touch of Class for a Grand Prix day. Joe believes that horses find their own way out of the ordinary routine, and when she started to win on a regular basis, Mill Pearl separated herself out from her contemporaries.

Left: Mill Pearl tucking up her front hooves and giving her all in response to Joe's demands at the Seoul Olympics, 1988.

Below: A sequence of photographs of a Mill Pearl training session. Joe is on Mill Pearl, Conrad is watching.

Far right: Joe makes a fluent jump on George Lindemann's Night Fever in the practice arena at West Palm Beach in 1989.

Below: Joe and Touch of Class at West Palm Beach, 1989. Touch of Class was the mare who helped Joe realize every show-jumper's dream: to win both team and individual gold medals, as he did at the Los Angeles Olympics in 1984. Sensitive handling and a cool, calm approach – no matter how the nerves might be jangling – proved the key to victory in Los Angeles for Joe on this former racehorse.

Joe's evaluation of Mill Pearl's gaits is at odds with the basic rule of thumb that they must all be good. "One great asset is an excellent mind. She has a correct way of thinking for our purposes and is very trusting. Any direction I point her in she goes, saying, 'Okay Joe.' As the work progresses, her nature is to become more anxious and hotter." Joe counteracts this tendency by working the mare quite slowly and peacefully, being sure not to add too much stress, even to flatwork, in which he employs a coaxing approach.

At about 7 o'clock on the morning of a Nations' Cup or Grand Prix, Mill Pearl is worked on the flat. Later, her groom, Hob Power, gives her 20 to 30 minutes' walking. When Joe has walked the course, she is given a few jumps. The aim is to provide a peaceful preparation.

Touch of Class requires a different approach because, as her work and the course progresses, she becomes harder to manage. But again, "The key to success is to keep the whole performance peaceful".

Joe and Conrad first came into contact with the mare, who belonged to one of their pupils, when she was seven years old, and became familiar with her through teaching when it became self-evident that she was very good.

In order to buy her, Joe and Conrad gathered together a consortium of owners – Mr and Mrs Patrick Butler, Mr Brownlee Currey and Mr Earl Mack. Sensibly, they retained a quarter share for themselves, represented by their Sandon enterprise.

One of the mare's strongest points was her precociousness. "Any way you headed her, she went. She also has a very strong character. A horse is not aware of its characteristics; we assign them, but they don't know."

The Los Angeles Olympics were the ultimate test for Touch of Class, and the first week that Joe spent with her at the Santa Anita Racetrack, where the show jumping was staged, did not augur well. Touch of Class had begun her days on the racetrack and, "Whether it's an asset or a detriment, horses have a great memory". On this occasion it was a detriment. The sight of the racetrack was all too much for the mare, and she was in a lather the whole time. "I thought, why am I here? These people are crazy to have sent me," recalls Joe. "Then, I was talking to Jimmy Williams [the highly renowned

Californian trainer], and explained that I was having a hard time and asked what I should do. He told me to school her every morning out of sight and away from the track, and it worked. I had a preconceived notion that it would be better to school by the track, but I was wrong; a quiet, far-distant corner was the answer.

"Soon she was jumping pleasantly in a soft, uncomplicated way from a trot and a canter. Calmness is a necessity; for example, it is silly to make a production about a shy at a mud puddle. It only compounds the horse's fear if you punish him and make him stand by the offending object, because you are making two negatives, which is bad."

As Joe's last two outstanding horses, Touch of Class and Mill Pearl, are both mares, it would be easy to assume that Joe favours mares, but this is not the case. He likes good horses irrespective of whether they are mares, stallions or geldings, and it is pure chance that his last two have been mares. But, "When a mare is good, she is usually very good; perhaps she has a touch more perception and a more sensitive feel than a gelding, and that tends to make the mare rather more special when she is already out of the ordinary. I think that mares try harder, but for themselves; I do not believe that they are trying their heart out for their rider. If a horse is presented with a problem in the shape of a jump in front of it, it tries to jump it in the best way possible. I think that is the vanity of the situation – self preservation."

Joe's and Conrad's present plan, of Conrad doing much of Joe's jumpers' flatwork, is masterly. Whenever he can, Joe watches Conrad riding to see what to do when he is in the saddle. He finds the horses always end up going very well on the flat after his friend has worked them. The sequel is that the horses then go better for Joe when he jumps them, so "It's a very positive move for me. Conrad always tries to watch me jump, and then afterwards we analyse what happened."

Despite the fact that by nature Joe is an over-rider and Conrad an under-rider, their types reverse when training. "I'd be very happy trotting over 3ft [0.9m] rails until the horses were 12 years old if left on my own. Conrad has to influence me as I'm a passive trainer and he is aggressive."

LESLIE BURR LENEHAN

From the very beginning, Leslie has had an innate talent, comparable to that of the Whitaker brothers, David Broome and Conrad Homfeld.

Horses work for her because she has a lovely touch and is generous, light and sympathetic. If a rider can give all these qualities to a horse, the horse invariably gives back. Even in her early days in ponies', hunters' and equitation finals, she had a wonderful inborn touch, not too formalized, rather casual in fact, but always with a great joie de vivre, *a happy attitude which reflects back through the horses she rides.*

She is very competitive, as tough and determined as any of the international riders, and on occasion can be overly so. I've tried to teach her that she need not take out a stride at the end of a course.

It's her spirit that is so wonderful. At the same time she is positive, active and aggressive. She dresses up a horse, giving it class and quality, decorating it in a totally different way.

George Morris

Leslie's greatest quality is that she is a winner. She may not be 100 per cent a stylist but she has such determination that there is not a class in the world that she cannot win.

Since she first made her mark on the international scene by winning the President's Cup at Washington in 1979 on Chase the Clouds, she has won almost all the sport's most glittering prizes. Only one short-term riding goal remains for her: the next World Championships.

In 1983 she was the American Grand Prix Association's (A.G.A.) Rider of the Year with Albany, Corsair and Boing, and in the winning U.S. team at the Pan-American Games with

Boing. A second team gold medal followed at the 1984 Olympics on Albany, then in 1986 she won the World Cup on McLain.

It is a dazzling record for a girl whose parents were actors who had had nothing to do with horses until their four-year-old daughter expressed an interest in ponies, when they leased her a Shetland.

Soon Leslie was galloping all day in a big Western saddle on the diminutive pony. Her parents decided that this wasn't quite right and that she should be properly trained. So she was sent to Tom and Sharon Hardy, who ran the local riding school at Highfields, Long Valley, New Jersey. When she was 14 years old, Tom began showing in international classes so Leslie, who already had a sound foundation, moved to be trained by George Morris. The following year she won the coveted Maclay Championship, and she stayed with George Morris for eight years.

George had the greatest influence on Leslie's career because, when she began to

Far left: Leslie Burr Lenehan and Pressurized competing at the West Palm Beach Grand Prix in 1989.

Left: Leslie is a rider with a good sense of humour – something that proves invaluable when travelling the long distances of the U.S. circuit.

field is a major equestrian enterprise. She gives lessons to her own clients and to other riders with their own horses, and she trains her own show jumpers, which usually number about eight and are at varying levels of development.

Fairfield is managed by Emerson Burr and his wife, Sari, Leslie and her husband, Brian Lenehan. None of the Burrs is related. Brian is a specialist hunter judge and show rider whose family tradition is steeped in horses. His father emigrated from Ireland in the 1930s, and his cousin runs the Firestone Stud near Dublin. Brian and Leslie were married in December 1984.

SELECTION

Leslie's favourite age for buying a horse is five or six years old. She now finds four a little too young and stays away unless "head over heels about the horse".

She has three equally important requirements: ability, carefulness and temperament. Regarding ability, she wants to know if the horse is athletic and able to clear a big jump. When considering a purchase, she has a fairly tight double set-up, high in with a tight distance inside and wide out. With this sequence, she can test if the horse has sufficient athletic capability.

Next, she wants to know if the horse is careful. "I love to see a horse's reaction when

Above: Leslie warming up on a hot day at West Palm Beach in 1989 – making the most of the Florida sunshine.

Right: Work continues whatever the weather: Leslie on a young horse in the mud at the Fairfield County Hunt Club.

ride for the U.S.E.T., Bert de Nemethy had left Gladstone and the American system had changed. Through George's teaching she developed what she considers "an immensely strong work ethic. Even now, I'll be teaching and hear him. He has such a system that you don't realize until later years that you have something to fall back on. Everything he taught me was so clear. For example, if a horse spooks, go towards the offending object and bend the horse's head away from it. He makes riding so simple and is not afraid to change. If your system isn't working, change it. So many people don't. Above all, he's very disciplined."

Leslie now lives at Westport, Connecticut, and works for the Fairfield County Hunt Club, which is barely 10 minutes' drive from her home. With seven barns and 150 horses, Fair-

he hits a jump. He could be too chicken. If he has a hard rub and hits the jump again, he's not careful. If he jumps lower, he's too much a chicken. If he jumps a foot higher with confidence, he's the one I want. I find Germans tend to be slow off the ground and scare themselves, then jump even lower the next time and maybe spook down at a Liverpool."

As far as temperament is concerned, Leslie's question is "Will the horse be trainable?", because some are too hot, crazy or stupid to learn. She always tries a horse twice. If she has to go back to basics again on the second day, she is not interested, because this means she would be wasting a lot of time.

Style is not crucial. "Albany performs amazing stunts with his legs to avoid rails, going a little to the right or left. And I don't mind a horse with a bad mouth. Albany's is bad but he's such a big winner." Ideally she looks for "a pretty blood horse who jumps in the classical way, but we've all had, or been very pleased to have, our McClains.

"I like a free mover and am not too hard on a horse who hangs his front legs a little, or one who twists, because it's one way of getting out of the way of a jump." Paul Schockemöhle's triple European Champion Deister's twisting style is a solid vindication of this latter statement.

Size is not a criterion. Although Leslie is a slender 5ft 6in (1.7m) tall, weighing 120lb (54kg), she is as happy on a horse of over 17

Left: Leslie – before the storm broke at the Fairfield County Hunt Club.

Below left: Leslie and Pressurized. Water ditches have been the graveyard of many hopes but here Pressurized, who can become over-excited, gives his rider full cooperation, and gets great height over this difficult fence.

hands high as she is on one of barely 16 hands high, such as her up-and-coming American thoroughbred, 911. "Small horses are usually the most agile and all right if they have matching scope and stride. I like a big horse that has a big stride and is clever. My only proviso is that he must be light. I have nothing against mares."

Carefulness rates as increasingly important with the trend towards lighter fences. "Today, course builders are becoming more and more sophisticated." Her Grand Prix horses all go in speed classes at some stage of their careers because "They are good for the rider and a confidence builder for the horse. Make no mistake, they helped to give Albany heart."

TRAINING

Leslie thoroughly enjoys teaching both horses and riders, such as Debbie Dolan or Megan Truman, and gets pleasure when she brings both or either through preliminary classes to Grand Prix. Many would describe her as determined, but she prefers to call herself stubborn.

Landman, who is by Landgraf, was foaled in 1982. When he arrived in the United States, he was jumping up to 4ft 9in (1.5m) and had a little spook. In general, she likes to school on a loose rein; on some horses she uses draw

reins and on others not. For jumping, the draw reins are shaped on to a breast plate for safety reasons, but on the flat they go back, between the forelegs under the brisket, on to the girth.

"I'm a forward rider; it's my nature," Leslie explains. "I like to ride with pace and get the horse going forwards, and my hands come in as they help to get the horse to lengthen and shorten. Landman is very supple. I work him quite a bit at the gallop because he can be dead to my legs going forward.

"Right now I'm working on transitions to help collect him; then I'll go forward again to cover all bases." Her horses must work well laterally and also in different positions of flexioning, with their heads low to stretch their top line and muscles.

Leslie uses this flexion to the ground in both collected and extended trotting because it is very good for the horse's muscles and conditions them. When she is training young riders, she does not let them use draw reins too soon because this could be dangerous.

Her priorities are three-fold: work in low flexion, high flexion and canter–gallop, the last because "That's where we all perform and win or lose classes. I don't understand people who spend hours on a tiny circle at sitting trot; it does nothing for a horse."

Leslie's philosophy is to jump a lot. She does not use big fences but her charges negotiate 20 or more minor jumps a day. She reasons, "They are not big, but fitness in show jumping is a major criterion, and I believe that if a horse's muscles aren't used every day – maybe just on Sunday, show day – the horse can't be fully conditioned". For Leslie, then, jumping is a daily occurrence. For example, Albany jumps every day of his life. She considers that that is why he is still young at 15 years old and as strong as ever.

In the outdoor arena there are seven fences from which to select. The overall basic height is 2ft 6in (0.8m) to 3ft (0.9m), and sometimes, at the end of a training session, 4ft (1.2m), but in this exercise height is not the name of the game.

The object is to keep the horses mentally alert, "always thinking there may be a jump just round the corner, and physically fit. If they only jump on Sundays at shows they can all too easily come out on Monday morning

Below: Leslie (standing left) giving a lesson to the fast-improving Megan Truman. Under Leslie's expert guidance Megan has brought her grey mare Gabby from preliminary up to Grand Prix standard.

feeling as though they have been run over by a train. Jumping demands more from the hind legs and increased stretching from the front legs, shoulders and front-end muscles."

Leslie's horses are rarely jumped over big fences at home. Four feet (1.2m) is her normal maximum and is not used all the time. Both her Grand Prix horses, Pressurized and Lenny, are very sound and need no medication; she is sure this is because of all the jumping they do. "The older I get, the more emphasis I put on fitness."

Landman is jumped on both leads and suddenly, before he realizes it, he is put diagonally into and over the second part of the double, an oxer over a Liverpool. Then he is brought back and put over the full double, without a moment's hesitation or resistance or a second look at the water. "This is an invaluable schooling fence for Landman because the entry is over white rails with natural scenery behind; it's very spooky and gives the horse a hard time sighting on the Liverpool behind. I caught him off guard and prevented the problem before he had it," explained Leslie. "I think it is the kiss of death to keep riding a horse by a fence he may find difficult or spooky. I might sometimes go into the arena but not close to the fence. When I bought Landman to the Liverpool for the first time, I turned my stick up well and made sure that I kept my rhythm. Often if the horse doesn't know where the problem is, it gets over the first time and the difficulty is the second time."

A LESSON

One of Leslie's students is Megan Truman, a promising 22-year-old rider who started her grey mare, Gabby, as a preliminary horse. She is now a considerable winner and to Leslie's delight made a successful Grand Prix debut at Palm Beach in the spring of 1988.

One of Gabby's main assets is that she is a great trier, which more than compensates for her long back and the fact that she jumps with a flat back rather than a rounded bascule.

Megan is working Gabby indoors because of a sudden storm of tropical intensity. Leslie encourages her to try to round Gabby's back on the flat to develop the mare's muscles. The aim is to keep Gabby contained in a tight

frame when she jumps, pushing her into a round shape and not hollowing in the air.

The second part of a double set against a wall, which is composed of low, dropped, crossed poles approached on the right rein, is the main jump of the lesson. Megan is trying to use her legs to decrease pace and compress Gabby. When using one element of a double to school, Leslie always selects the second, going-away part; this is to eliminate the possibility of the horse picking up the habit of stopping.

Above left: Most of Leslie's horses jump at least twenty relatively small fences each day as a means of keeping them well muscled up and fully fit.

Below: Jumping in the big school at the Fairfield County Hunt Club. The rug on the floor provides variety and ensures that the horse does not spook.

Above: Leslie warming up in the collecting ring at West Palm Beach. She includes transitions to help collect her horses prior to jumping.

Almost all horses are weaker off one side than the other, and Gabby is weaker off the right, which explains why Leslie is working her on that side. Leslie considers it important for a young rider to be aware and to feel whether the horse's back is rounded and if it is going straight.

At one of her jumps, Gabby skips off the ground rather than pushing off behind. Accordingly, Leslie encourages Megan to make sure that Gabby accepts both legs as she increases speed on the circle to the jump, then decreases speed on the approach and keeps well back.

The next jumping exercise is the reverse, a collected canter in the circle with increasing pace at the jump. "Avoid pitching your shoulders forward and relax or you will lose the frame," counsels Leslie. "Hold the approach, feel both reins and keep your shoulders back. When you turn a horse to a jump, it's very important that your shoulders are straight. It is better to jump first then turn; don't pull her back, and use equal pressure with both your reins and your legs.

"In a jump-off, when tight turns are needed, you must get the horse very well balanced. On a sharp right turn you may often feel the pulling on the rein and lose the left-hand side. This can be avoided if the horse can jump up easily from the hocks; the rider can influence this by being sure both hands and legs are ex-

erting equal pressure and that her weight is evenly distributed. This should ensure you don't let the horse get heavy on either side or out of balance and out of line."

Megan then successfully jumps from both a sharply cut and a straight approach, keeping her shoulders straight. Then she tries a shorter turn in, "more a jump-off situation. Go get it; don't be so tentative. Cut in and push," advises Leslie.

"Whilst it is better to jump off the correct lead, it is not imperative. Albany can jump well off a cross canter; he switches to the left lead. Joe Fargis's Touch of Class, who carried him to the Olympic team and individual gold medals at the 1984 Olympic Games, was always changing."

Now Megan tackles the full double, which is 2ft (0.6m) wide. Her instructions are "Jump in and out and back and forth. Get more of a line back from the mouth." Megan tends to drop her hands after the jump, Leslie notes. "Keep them wider and higher; use more knee pressure after the jump and relax. Don't be so restricted."

When the jump is raised to 4ft (1.2m), more punch is necessary at the base. Gabby goes much better and higher off her near fore and has a real lead change problem. Megan is encouraged to gallop and relax more after the second jump and told not to change her approach in, anticipating punching out over the second part. "Off the right rein, support with your leg so she doesn't lean right.

"I'm always saying that it's hard work for the show-jumping horses and much easier for the hunters. A horse has to be much fitter to show jump; let's face it, I couldn't go out and win the Boston Marathon. I'm stubborn; at first I didn't say this but now I know it's absolutely right."

TRAINING ALBANY

Debbie Dolan's Albany had his final school from Leslie before flying to England for his owner to ride at the Hickstead Nations' Cup meeting in June, 1989.

Leslie has a great respect for Albany because he always goes into the ring to win. She considers him to be a great horse, using the yardstick that if he is going well, he can be ridden by many different riders. Conversely,

she thinks that Conrad Homfeld's 1984 Olympic team gold and individual silver-medal-winning partner, Abdullah, only went consistently for him – a tribute to Conrad's horsemanship. In contrast, Albany went well for his early rider, Jo-Anne Kovacs, Leslie, Debbie Dolan and also Rodney Jenkins in a chance one-off ride.

It is all a matter of knowing and comprehending your horse. Whatever Albany is doing, he has a wonderful interest and is full of vitality with a playful manner. There is never a mean kick-out, and it is clear that he enjoys life and is a happy horse.

Albany usually has a warm-up of at least 20 minutes' duration – longer than is usual for a younger horse because Leslie finds that the older horses get, the more they need to stretch out slowly through high and low flexions and to the left and right at both short and long gaits. She feels that once the resistance and stiffness have gone, Albany is ready to work in the areas of lateral schooling and gait.

Leslie emphasizes that when warming up a top international horse, her four basic principles are to work high and low at both extended gaits and to stretch out fully to both sides freely and with suppleness. To achieve the latter, she does a lot of lateral work.

Albany is worked on the flat with long draw reins going back to the girth through his front legs, and is put through his paces, according to Leslie's four principles, in straight lines, circles of different diameter and various other figures, at all gaits. For reasons already described, shoulder-in and lateral work are the priorities.

"He chooses to jump all his fences off the left lead and is better off it. He's stiff on his left side; he always has been. You must find out your horse's imperfections and work at them. You need to know the feel of your horse and to know that horses vary."

Albany's jumping practice builds up to a double of oxers taken in both directions. His rug has been placed under one in an endeavour to make it spooky and simulate a Liverpool. Halfway through the session, the navy and gold Fairfield livery rug is turned over, its stripier side uppermost to try and throw him – unsuccessfully, as it turns out. "I used it to make him take a peek but not spook." This diversion was because Leslie considers Hickstead to be an impressive ring.

The last time Albany had jumped was just three days earlier in the Old Salem Grand Prix. The going there was very deep after a sudden torrential rainstorm – which held up the competition halfway through. Leslie's final exceptionally demanding combination and the double with the additional hazard of the rug were precautionary measures for similar tests that might be set at Hickstead.

Leslie considers that the top course designers are becoming more and more sophisticated and that they are armed with a far greater range of equipment. "Just think," she says, "what Bert de Nemethy did at the World Cup Final in 1989: a long distance into a triple set close to a wall with a high third pole which needed big clearance behind".

PRESSURE

One of the secrets of Leslie's ongoing success is her combination of hard work and determination. She is unhappy if she is not working with horses, and does not feel pressure from competition. "I'm not nervous, I never have been, but in another sense I do feel pressure because I have such wonderful owners and I want to do well for them."

Frank Chapot laughingly calls her "a bit scatty; I've known her miss the starting bell. As a trainer and *chef d'équipe* I have to remind her, 'Listen out for the horn, but don't go through the start until it sounds; and remember, the last jump is number 12 not number 11.' If we are flying to, say, Brussels and put down in London on the way, I have to be sure she's brought her passport. She's a lovely person, a very tough competitor. She can just ride in and nail European riders of the highest class, such as Nick Skelton and Paul Schockemöhle."

Leslie agrees with these comments: "I do occasionally have problems going off course; I have to go over my course ten times. I can all too easily get one-tracked and forget where the start is. I'm tunnel visioned. To me the sequence of jumps is irrelevant. I get so interested in how my horse is going."

"At the Los Angeles Olympic Games, when I arrived in our barn on the day of the Prix des Nations," recounts Chapot, "Leslie flew by several times looking very flurried. She'd forgotten her breeches and was waiting desperately for someone to bring them. I'd say that's a little typical."

Above: Leslie jumping Pressurized at the West Palm Beach Grand Prix, 1989: "This is a situation I try to avoid. His centre of gravity is a little too far forward and he's rolling over his front end, pitching it forward too much."

Right: Leslie and Pressurized in the Nations' Cup, Calgary, 1989: "Pressurized's front legs are uneven, but he is demonstrating good balance and a 'round' bascule over the jump."

FAVOURITE HORSES

Chase the Clouds, the floating grey who launched Leslie on her international career and then, sadly, died of colic, fits firmly into this category. Currently, Leslie gives Debbie

Dolan's American thoroughbred, Pressurized, an estimable rating. When Debbie offered Leslie the ride, she was more than happy to accept because she has a high regard for Pressurized. She also much appreciated Debbie's offer because at the time she lacked a truly top-class, experienced international horse.

Pressurized, who was foaled in 1979, is a lovely, very tight type of show jumper. His only problem is that he is ultra-careful, so gets easily scared, which can affect his confidence and rideability if he makes an error.

In 1989, on the Florida Sunshine Circuit, when he won the Palm Beach Grand Prix, the picture was perfect. Then, at the Tampa Invitational, Leslie did not manage to come into the testing combination as she had planned, and Pressurized "flipped the final and third element, pitching me on to the ground". Because he is ultra-sensitive, the effects of this incident carried over and he stopped in the World Cup Final at Tampa one and a half weeks later. "Now I think that if I'd realized how profoundly upset he was, I would have schooled him much longer immediately prior to the World Cup Final."

At the time it is not always easy to discover how upset a horse has been by such an incident. On the second day, Pressurized had the third fence, a skinny vertical. He was then third in the third and final World Cup round, "because I set to and he was really looking and knew just what to do".

In 1988 Leslie rode Pressurized with a long rein. Now she uses a shorter rein with a smaller frame, which she finds more effective. "My approach has changed. As George Morris always says, 'If something isn't working, change the formula.'"

In 1989 Pressurized proved more consistent, and in every school he has he is given some "hard college work. With his intricate mind, great sensitivity and ultra-carefulness, it is all too easy for him to make a telling mistake if he has not got both a mental and physical balance."

Leslie has a special affection for Lenny, who she sold to Mrs Jane F. Clarke in April 1989 while retaining the ride. "He's my pet; the only one I've ever owned who has reached Grand Prix level." Lenny, who was foaled in 1981, was bought as a six-year-old and is "the craziest horse I've ever worked with, even at a straightforward walk, trot and canter. Initially he was very head shy; it took me half an hour to put on the bridle the first time I tried."

Lenny is by Paul Schockemöhle's stallion Geppart. Away from the show ring he is very affectionate with lots of personality. "When he finally arrived off the plane, I'd hoped that Brian might buy a share in him, but he looked rough and shaggy, and Brian declined."

By 1988 Lenny was physically stronger, because Leslie had spent hours and hours working him. She looks back: "I think the German system is long and heavy, but although Lenny is a German, he is a thoroughbred in disguise. You'd think he'd be sluggish, but he is more of a thoroughbred than any horse I've ever ridden."

His style of going suits that of Leslie's riding because he responds to a light seat and hand. He, too, is super careful with all the scope in the world and he is not spooky. He is one of the quickest horses on his feet that Leslie has ever ridden, able to gallop very quickly to a jump and pick up instantly. But there remains much re-education to be done: "It would be much better if he had not been broken in at all than broken in in the way he was".

Frank Chapot manages Mrs Clarke's horses, so Lenny spends much of his time away from shows at Frank's Neshanic Station home in New Jersey. "This provides a good change of scene for him. Frank's groundwork and the chance to be turned out and to relax in the surrounding fields couldn't be better."

Below: Leslie and Corsair, West Palm Beach Grand Prix, 1983. "This is very typical of Corsair: a perfect front end, legs even and quick, his long back a little hollow. He wants to cut down at his back end and, although he's in the middle of the jump, he's already on his way down. He always saved time in the air and never wanted to jump over the back rail of an oxer."

KATIE MONAHAN PRUDENT

Katie is the greatest all-round woman rider I've ever seen. She's as powerful as any man, including Gerd Wiltfang – both powerful and dominating. Like few men, however, she can be powerful and strong yet in the same breath be delicate, first driving over a fence and then, light as a feather and sympathetic, doing almost nothing over the next. Her range is tremendous.

She has a good, deep seat and a great hunter background – a hunter forward-seat rider after the same ideology as myself. I consider her a master technician and second to none in this sphere.

George Morris

Katie is one of the United States' most successful show jumpers ever, with many victories to her credit from more than a decade on a wide variety of horses. She was the American Grand Prix Association Rider of the Year in 1982, 1986 and 1988, and to date is the only rider to have won this title three times in the United States. In 1982, 1985 and 1988 she rode the leading U.S. Horse of the Year, respectively Noren, The Governor and Special Envoy.

An exceptional year was 1988, perhaps her best yet. Riding Special Envoy she narrowly missed becoming the first-ever rider to capture the United States' triple crown, winning the Michelob American Invitational for a record third time and the Invitational Jumping Derby for a second straight season, then being placed second, by 0.2 seconds, in the final leg, the American Gold Cup.

Katie's parents had no equestrian connections, but from an early age she loved horses. They bought her a quarter horse, Tina, who was a former barrel racing champion and who, because of her early occupation, could balance herself and catch the young Katie if

necessary, thus instilling confidence in her at a crucial age.

Soon Katie was the Michigan State Junior Equitation Champion, already seeking and developing the certain style, accuracy and correct position that characterises her riding today. She also started hunting, which made her consider how a horse jumps and how to achieve balance in good style. Most Europeans are not aware of creating style, and that today in the United States it is possible to create great riders out of non-natural riders through the superb coaching that is readily available, especially if the would-be international has a sizeable bank balance. "The only problem for the current crop of such stylish, accurate and very successful riders is that when their horses spook, whirl or rear, they are stuck."

No matter how great and talented, every rider needs a touch of luck to get his or her feet on to the first rung of the ladder, and Katie's parents inadvertently provided this

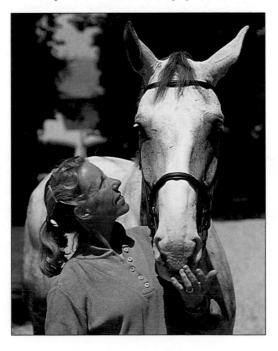

Far left: Katie and Nordic Venture giving a fence enormous clearance at Stockholm in 1989. Katie was jumping there in preparation for the place she hoped to win in the U.S. team for the 1990 World Championships. Unfortunately, a head injury sustained the preceding spring prevented her from being considered for the team. She still intends to try for the 1992 Olympic Games.

Left: A nuzzle for Katie from a very affectionate Nordic Venture.

Above: Katie and Make My Day at Rosières aux Salines in France, June, 1989.

when they bought a house in Bloomfield Hills across the street from the local riding club. From the very beginning, "Every movement I have made with horses, my parents have been very supportive," recalls Katie, "and this has been the most enormous help".

Before she was ready for more educated, polished and sophisticated training, she had three invaluable early instructors in Michigan. First, Bob Egan and John Slaughter, who she rates as "great equitation coaches; they gave me position and style and drilled me on how to control horses when I was 10, 11 and 12 years old. At this stage I spent hours learning basic essentials, such as how to go on three strides on the right lead, then three strides on the left lead, how to stop correctly and how to turn on a dime."

Bill Queen was Katie's next instructor, in her early teens. An old-style Virginia horseman, he and his wife trained young horses, and Katie learnt from them what it takes to start a youngster. "Even now, things they taught me flood back when I am breaking young horses."

Former international and now course designer Chrystine Jones Tauber is a little older than Katie but has been a friend since Katie's early days. When she left the U.S.E.T., she was instrumental in furthering the then 14-year-old Katie's flatwork and basic dressage with lessons by the hour, concentrating on such movements as extensions and improving Katie's seat and legs.

Katie then had the valuable opportunity of riding show hunters, which to this day remains a great love. She thoroughly enjoyed competing with the much more experienced Christine that August and September at the North Shore and Piping Rock Shows on Long Island for Sally Sexton. The latter, the grand dame of the United States hunter world, lived in Ohio and now lives in Virginia, where she breeds thoroughbreds. This proved another stroke of luck, because "One day Sally said to me, 'If you are ever going to win a class for me, you need a lesson with George Morris', and she arranged my first lesson and paid for it". The year was 1969, and the following November, when she was only 15 years old and by then under George's tutelage full time, Katie triumphed in the coveted Maclay Championship in Madison Square Garden at the New York Horse Show.

"I've continued with George for the rest of my life," elaborates Katie. "He's incredible; a great motivator and a wonderful teacher. No matter what happens, he keeps his riders looking forward with interest to the future, and this is a considerable part of the battle."

Katie spent 12 years with George, and it was not until 1981, when she started her own enterprise, that she cut her direct ties with him, although she remains secure in the knowledge that if she needs advice, he is there to help her. She will never forget the support and advice he gave her to actually get into the ring on a competitive basis.

Her base is Plain Bay Farm at Middleburg, Virginia. 'Plain Bay' is a common term in the United States but not in Europe. It means a bay with no (or only a diminutive amount of) white about him. Katie chose the name because she has had so many good plain bays, among them The Jones Boy (who carried her into second place behind Hugo Simon and Gladstone at the inaugural Volvo World Cup Final in Gothenburg in 1979), Bullwinkle, a thoroughbred Grand Prix jumper owned by her family, and her first good jumper–hunter, Milltown.

Katie counts herself fortunate to have been on Bert de Nemethy's final European tour in 1980, when she was riding Silver Exchange and was a member of the U.S. team which finished fifth in the alternative Olympic Games at Rotterdam. "I developed a great respect for Bert, although he was not crazy about girls in those early days. He softened after the Melanie Smith era but always did a marvellous job organizing."

SELECTION

Katie really likes to deal with young horses, but to go into competition herself she looks at the six-, seven- and eight-year-old range, because by that age the horses have some experience. "My strong suit is that I can give a horse confidence. I have an accurate eye and am an aggressive rider. I have had fun choosing difficult horses and bringing them on with success. Perhaps that's the overall reason that I have not been more successful internationally. In other countries or continents – compare Europe with the U.S. – things change under different conditions, and when horses are worried or feel a little out of their depth, they tend to slide back to their former problems."

Katie does not consider herself a real stickler for type and does not judge on looks, but she likes to see a horse jump. First and foremost, it must jump in a fairly correct style and

Above: Katie and Teddy, West Palm Beach, 1989: "This was Teddy's second year as a jumper; he's a real winner and is going very high over the fence, really sailing. However good a rider is, he can't give a horse the instinct to get over a fence and clear it. What Teddy lacks in ability he makes up for in heart and try."

Left: Katie and Make My Day at Hickstead, 1987. For Katie, "this is a typical picture. He's a classical style jumper; no matter how you get there, you can always count on him to jump in perfect style. As I'm from a hunter background, I'm concerned about the style of a horse when it jumps."

When Katie goes to see a horse, she likes to watch it being ridden and jumped before she tries it herself. "I'd be more comfortable picking a horse watching someone else riding than riding myself if I couldn't do both. I'm very relaxed and have the confidence to give horses rein, which can improve a horse very fast. For choice when I ride, I'd just set up a combination for myself to test scope.

"I hope the other rider will make an error because I can then learn a lot from how the horse reacts and what he does. If I sense the horse has a hole, I try to expose it; for example, by setting a very tight vertical if I think he is slow in front, or, if the horse seems spooky, I might put a jacket on a fence and see what he makes of that."

Katie flew three times to Britain to try Nordic Venture but "I could not find a hole anywhere. Nordie is not very pretty, he's a big heavy German in both type and character, but like a thoroughbred to ride. When I first saw his big head I thought, 'What am I doing here?' Now I realize that his head may be ugly but he has a very intelligent look in his eyes, although his left eye is a little sleepy. He is no beauty but he is both smart looking and smart, which is much more important."

Above: Katie and Special Envoy at the water at Hickstead, 1987: "'Special' is very brave and has had lots of success over Derby-type terrains. He is at his best in a field like Hickstead, where everything is big and impressive."

Right: Katie on the powerful Nordic Venture. Katie admits that "Nordie is not very pretty, he's a big heavy German in both type and character, but like a thoroughbred to ride".

have scope; then, if it is careful, her second major condition has been met. She used not to look too strongly for temperament and character but does so now because these attributes are vitally important as regards the Olympic Games, which are now her major target. Additionally, but by no means least, a horse must want to do its job.

Secondary considerations include how brave and careful a horse is. Bravery and carefulness together are "the perfect combination, but these two qualities don't always mix because a brave horse may rub a jump and a careful horse can be too timid".

Size is not a criterion. Of Katie's current top three horses, Special Envoy stands under 16 hands high while Make My Day and Nordic Venture are "quite tall"; in fact the latter is certainly not less than 17 hands high. However, her horses must all move well and have a big stride, which Katie considers usually comes with scope. "I certainly don't lock into type; think of Jappeloup, who is just over 15 hands high."

She does not care if a horse is a thoroughbred or a warmblood, but likes sensitive horses and hates dull ones. "French horses are famous for having bad mouths, but I believe it's because of the way they are started." Of her three current best horses, Make My Day is a thoroughbred and Special Envoy and Nordic Venture are warmbloods. Special Envoy is a Hanoverian, while Nordic Venture is well bred by show-jumping standards, being by the Oldenburg stallion Gotthard out of a French dam who is by the Anglo-Arab Colorado.

One of Colorado's other offspring, incidentally, is Michael Whitaker's puissance specialist (with 16 wins by October, 1990) and Grand Prix winner, Didi.

Nordic Venture

Although it is early days, Katie thinks that there is every possibility that Nordic Venture will prove her best-ever horse. Throughout her career she has been careful with her clients' money and never spent a fortune on her purchases; but she spent more on Nordic Venture because her great objective is the 1992 Olympic Games.

Despite her superb record in the United States, she analyses, "At international level my success is sometimes lacking, and I realize that a very special horse is needed for the Games, not an everyday winner. If a horse has a hole it may well be possible to get over it at lesser competitions but not at the Games. Nordic Venture has no problems; he is a sound, young ten-year-old."

When Katie bought Nordic Venture in early 1989, on behalf of Mr and Mrs Bertram Firestone, he had been brought to international level by his then owner–producer, Fergus Graham, and Fergus's former wife, Paula, with their customary care and thoroughness. Most importantly, he had not been pushed on to the next stage before he was ready. The next projects in his development were to further his international experience and gradually to teach him to go fast against the clock but not to try to go full out in order to win Grand Prix.

Young and inexperienced internationally as he is, one reason that Katie thinks he is so promising is that the only mistakes he makes are through his greenness, "being wandery and looking out of the ring, but never because he's not trying or thinking of not doing his job.

Left: A practice jump for Katie and Nordic Venture at Old Salem in May, 1989. Katie's husband Henri looks on.

Sometimes horses are tense, nervous or belligerent or don't want to be ridden, but he has so much ability that it is easy for him and he is never flustered."

Katie's first competitions with Nordic Venture were in the United States, and in May 1989 she was encouraged when she won her first Grand Prix with him at Farmington, in Connecticut.

TRAINING

Later in May at Old Salem, Connecticut, the lake alongside the beautiful bowl-type arena caused many horses of all levels of experience and education to spook and lose their concentration. "Nordie is very enthusiastic about his jumping but not hot, he just loves to go; so because he is that type of horse, he has been held back initially, not driven, and now the time has come when he has to be driven forward."

The weather deteriorated fast during the Old Salem Grand Prix, with the wind whipping round and torrential rain lashing down. The sudden storm was just reaching its climax as Katie's turn to enter the arena with Nordic Venture came.

An early spook meant a rail down; then, at the optional line towards the lake, Katie pushed him forward to cut a stride, and Nordic Venture veered and missed it. "He got to it impossibly long and he had it down quite hard, which upset him because he is sensitive. I hurried him because at that stage of the competition no one was clean. The wind rushed, the rain pelted down and everything came up so fast. It was a horrid mess. Then the tree by the jump at the end of the course blew down, and we totalled eight faults."

Old Salem was to have been the grey's last show before travelling to Europe, but as Katie had only been competing with him for two months, she felt she did not know him well enough. So, as their last competitive experience together had not been an auspicious one, she changed her plans and took him to the Devon County Show.

There she planned to ride him only in small classes, looking for option fences where she could leave out a stride as the essential practice at that time. The Grand Prix was definitely not on Nordic Venture's schedule, but when the horse that Katie had entered in the Grand Prix went lame at the last minute, she again changed her plans and started him.

Below: Katie and Nordic Venture, West Palm Beach, 1989. "Here's a beautiful jump in the ring [left], where Nordic Venture is obviously waiting and listening. I'm starting to turn in the air and he's right with me, ready for the next jump. [In the centre picture] he still looks as though he's listening and ready to do whatever I ask. Here [right] he's coming back to the rider's hands, but in such a supple way that it doesn't affect his hind end in the air; there is no suggestion of stiffness."

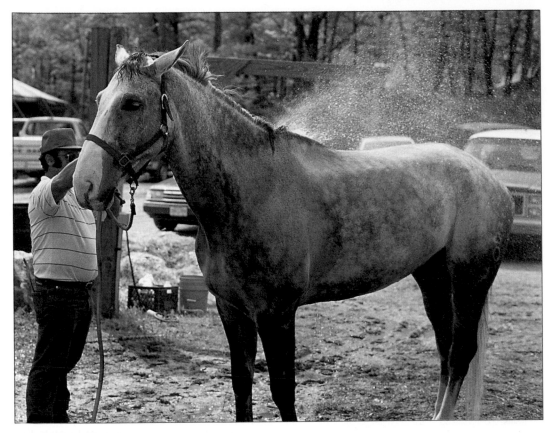

The combination reached the final jump-off, where they had the sixth and final draw. "The early horses had gone so quickly that I didn't go for a blazer, but I was fastish and very pleased to finish sixth." The pair then left for Europe, and after a week at the farm of Katie's husband, Henri, to get ready, when Henri helped by riding Nordie a little for Katie on the flat, they departed for Aachen.

The West German Mecca is one of Katie's favourite venues: the big, impressive courses and the electric, almost Olympic, atmosphere provide one of the greatest tests in the world. Nordic Venture's second placing in the Grand Prix to Franke Sloothaak's and Paul Schockemöhle's experienced Walzerkönig proved to Katie that her judgement had been right. In the Grand Prix she rode him without spurs or a stick, and she returned to France with her confidence boosted and the knowledge that her immediate priority must be training for increased speed.

Katie finds working at most European shows more difficult than in the U.S. because overall they offer much less space. In the States, most shows have extensive facilities available, such as at Lake Placid, which she rates as superb with its five different schooling areas, all of which are supervised, and a wide selection of practice jumps.

She believes that Special Envoy's form in Europe in the summer of 1989, which was disappointing, "can be attributed to the relatively cramped European warm-up facilities. He tends to be aggressive and needs large areas for schooling, general areas in which I can get him to relax. Shows like Franconville, Cannes and Zürich, with scant jumps and a lack of space, make this very difficult."

Nordic Venture was also not best suited to Franconville for another reason. "The stands were small and in the ring it seemed to be all edges, and there were a lot of people. It was all very different for Nordie; he looked out and didn't concentrate on the course. Other than this tendency, which I can control and improve, he has all the qualities necessary to become a consistent winner. And later on, of

129

Right: Katie schooling Nordic Venture: "He's a beautiful mover, and you don't get that feeling at all when you see this big powerful horse in the stable".

Below: Nordic Venture watches Katie's dog, Villy, as he enjoys a cooling rest in the river that bounds the work-out field at Rosières aux Salines.

course, he settled well in Zürich, where he was seventh in the Grand Prix."

Katie's first baby, Adam, arrived according to a carefully worked out schedule on 27 December, 1989. She originally planned to be back in action in the spring of 1990 on the Florida Circuit but a severe head injury put paid to that. She now plans to try for the 1992 Olympic Games if she feels 100 per cent fit.

Selection in the U.S. in World Championships and Olympic Games years is a problem. "Sometimes the trials get like the Olympics themselves, and I worry about this because we are so busy competing with each other for team places that we can all too easily over-jump before the Games. I've got to a point now where I can peak my horses for a major competition and know exactly what it takes to get them ready."

Working Nordic Venture

Musing as she warms up Nordic Venture, Katie says, "He's a beautiful mover, and you don't get that feeling at all when you see this big powerful horse in the stable. He is also very balanced when he pings off the ground; he is like elastic. There is all that power, but you don't hear the pounding of hooves like you did with my stallion Noren's explosive take-off." By July, 1989, the grey was much more muscled up than ever before, especially across his quarters and loins.

The field where Katie's husband, Henri, used to school his horses is bordered by a languishing, deep-set green river, and is filled with Three-Day-Event-orientated jumps. These are excellent for show jumpers, because they force the horse to keep alert.

Villy, Katie's grey Schnauzer dog, watches his mistress negotiate the two-tiered bank from all conceivable angles with consummate ease. Then Nordie loses concentration when asked to jump a fallen tree trunk alongside the water, and he spooks one way because of looking at the meandering water of the river where it catches the light. He is put over it several times and reminded to pay attention and pick up his feet.

A small green oxer is the next target, not unlike the infamous Hickstead privet oxer, of which the victims include no less than triple European champions Paul Schockemöhle and Deister, George Morris, and Katie herself with Make My Day.

At his first attempt, Nordie tries to bank it because he mistakes it for a bank and puts down his front legs in the centre top, hastily retracting them. "We don't have a whole lot of privet oxers in the States but plenty of banks," explains Katie. "He thought it was a bank; it looks very similar on approach to a grass-topped one."

At his ensuing attempts, Nordie puts his hind legs down on the oxer but eventually desists and jumps clean, whereupon Katie has a pole put in the centre to be absolutely certain that the distinction between bank and oxer has been firmly established in Nordie's mind.

"I don't like to get a rub in the schooling area with a careful horse; you can almost teach such a horse to get a rub. I might, before a second Grand Prix jump-off in the collecting ring, but not often. I think it is a mistake to make a horse rub too much."

After a refreshing bareback walk in the river, Katie pops Nordic Venture over his first ever Bullfinch (a hedge topped by tall, thin twigs), and he picks up very high. "I've always wanted to jump in a bareback puissance," she jokes, "but I'm too chicken, although I am a Badminton bird [i.e. a shuttlecock]. If I fall, I land on my *derrière*; then I bounce up again."

The mark of a good rider is to succeed on many horses, not just one, which in Katie's case is perfectly illustrated by her current three top horses, all of whom are infinitely different in type.

Of these three horses, Make My Day – Maker for short – is Katie's favourite. "He is like a little child; so timid, but careful. I enjoy giving him confidence. Things that happened back in his past stop him from being an Olympic or great horse because he can very easily get scared, but he showed his ability by winning a ribbon in every class at Aachen in 1989.

"The French word *retive* describes Maker well. As a young horse, before I had him, he had some bad rides, and when I first rode him he reared in corners. As he is very careful, he sometimes preferred to say no. There is so much more to success than just riding. I love to figure out a horse's mentality."

Katie excels in dealing with problem horses for this very reason, and also because

of her ability to discover their mental approach and to judge their potential: she is able to empathise with, and so to encourage, them. "Sometimes I feel rather like a schoolmistress."

Special Envoy is a complete contrast. "He's not really a likeable individual, gets cranky, pins his ears and swishes his tail." She finds that he responds well to Henri riding him on the flat, which puts him in a good frame of mind. When he goes badly, as in 1989 in Europe, it spurs Katie on rather than discouraging her.

Below: Make My Day at West Palm Beach. Katie comments that "My job is to bolster his confidence because he is so timid".

Above: Katie clearing a big spread on Bean Bag at West Palm Beach.

Right: Make My Day making little of a vertical with no ground line in the practice arena at West Palm Beach.

Fred wanted to import French horses; Henri, who enjoyed buying and selling, went to work for him for a year. He met Katie at the Virginia State Horse Show, where she was riding the French stallion Noren, formerly known as Gaisier de Fleury.

Her marriage to a European made Katie increasingly aware that although she was extremely successful in the United States, her results wcre not as consistently good in Europe. This presented a vitalizing new challenge, one more demanding than staying at the top at home and, as a true professional, Katie determined to analyse why her international record did not match her national record and to try to remedy the situation.

Having a base on either side of the Atlantic was the key to the project she and Henri envisaged. Katie's Plain Bay Farm at Middle-

The key to success with Mrs Pamela Harriman's Special Envoy – named after the appointment of her late husband, Averil Harriman, as special envoy to Russia – is to keep him relaxed mentally.

MARRIAGE ACROSS THE WATER

Marriage changes anyone's life in some way, but Katie's marriage to Frenchman Henri Prudent, in December, 1986, was to have a profound influence on her show-jumping career. In 1989 she became the prototype of the jet-setting show jumper, spending the summer commuting between one string of show jumpers and hunters and her pupils in the U.S. and another string of show jumpers based in France. Were she not married to Henri, it is most unlikely that this situation would have arisen.

Henri was brought up at Rosières aux Salines, south-east of Nancy, where his mother, Annette, still lives. He is a former member of the French Three Day Event team and used to school his horses at the National Stud, which is one of the oldest in France and houses 30 stallions, from thoroughbreds and Anglo-Arabs to Ardennais.

He was always very interested in show jumpers, and after working for Swiss dealer Gerhard Etter moved to the United States to work for Fred Graham, who owned a farm in Virginia and, at the time, the stallion Almay.

burg, Virginia, comprises 20 stalls set round a small, 19th-century stone house. There are usually some 15 or 20 horses there, and Katie rates it the perfect size and finds it easy to shut down when, for example, she moves south to compete on the Florida Circuit each February. Complications with her students are allayed because most of them have their own stables and grooms and meet her at shows, with occasional visits to Plain Bay Farm as necessary.

Henri's dealing business is conveniently based at Beau Rose Farm, some 30 minutes' drive from Charles de Gaulle Airport, south-east of Paris, near Ozoire. Although he sells 'special' horses to the United States, this is an excellent site for developing young horses; furthermore, there is a bigger market for average horses in Europe, so he does more dealing in France than America. Katie has found that one advantage of jumping in Europe is that it is cheaper to compete.

The very welcome opportunity to use some of the stables at Rosières aux Salines provides an excellent base for shows not only in eastern France, but at venues such as Luxembourg. The atmosphere, deep in the Lorraine countryside near Nancy, is very restful, and there is the welcome variety of the horse trials jumps for schooling and fenced turning-out areas.

Katie's daunting 1989 transatlantic schedule began at Rome in May. She then flew back to the States for Farmington and Old Salem in Connecticut, also in May, then on to Devon County before crossing to Aachen, Germany, in June. Next it was back to France for Franconville, north-west of Paris, west over the Atlantic again to Lake Placid, back east to Switzerland for the Zürich Grand Prix, then a rest at Rosières aux Salines. Finally there was the three-country, three-week trip to Luxembourg, Stockholm and Dinard in July and August, before the return to home in Virginia to rejoin the American circuit.

On many of her flights Katie is cushioned in Mr Firestone's private jet, which helps her defeat jet lag. "It's just like a luxury hotel in the air, with a bed and first-class service." When Katie travels on a regular service, she is careful to book her flight sufficiently ahead of the show to allow at least one day's sleep before competing.

Katie says that the two people who have helped most in realizing her jet-set show-jumping ambitions are her husband, Henri, and her Mexican groom, Pancho Lopez. "I'm a very intense, competitive person, and, for a start, they both have mellow, kind dispositions and keep me on the right track. When Pancho quits, I quit," she says. Pancho, who comes from the idyllic Pacific coast resort of Puerta Vallerta, concurs, but with the proviso "I hope that won't be soon". She rates Pancho "a genius with horses and able to keep them very sound, however tough their schedule".

Above left and above: Katie and her husband, Henri, walk a course together – and discuss the problems it poses. The couple first met at the Virginia State Horse Show, and married in December, 1986.

133

ANNE KURSINSKI

Realizing that she could not advance her international career any further without the more competitive atmosphere to be found on the United States' eastern seaboard, Anne moved from California to Hunterdon Inc., my riding establishment in New Jersey, where she has been for a decade, dividing her time between her own jumpers and teaching. During this time she has won both team and individual gold medals at the 1983 Pan-American Games on Livius and a team silver medal at the 1988 Olympic Games on Starman. She was also a reserve for the 1984 Olympics.

Week to week Anne is very consistent, and she rises to the occasion when the chips are down. She is a very high-class rider for championship competitions. She manages her horses and schedules very well and knows when, and when not, to jump.

The Californian trainer Jimmy Williams made Anne with a strong emphasis on dressage, which is in her favour. She has ridden up to Dressage Grand Prix standard and hopes one day to return to this discipline. Because of her initial training, she is as strong on the flat as any girl or man, both schooling and working well. Her position does not exactly reflect my teaching because she does not have as much of a forward seat as I advocate.

George Morris

A native Californian who was born in Pasadena on 16 April, 1959, Anne had Jimmy Williams as one of her early mentors. She has also competed in dressage and in the future may well return to this discipline on a serious level. She is renowned for her fluid American style and pleasant, calm personality. Her skill as a rider peaked in Korea at the 1988 Olympic Games when riding the Westfalian stallion Starman; on that occasion she was a member of the U.S. silver-medal-winning team. She also tied for fourth in the individual jumping with Britain's David Broome and Countryman.

She first rode for the U.S.E.T. in 1978, and in 1983, riding Livius, won the individual gold medal and fronted the U.S. gold-medal-winning team at the Pan-American Games in Caracas, Venezuela. She has been in winning Nations' Cup teams at major international venues such as Aachen, Hickstead, Calgary and Rome.

In 1988 she was voted the A.H.S.A. Audi Horsewoman of the Year, and she is a firm campaigner for safer headwear. Since moving east she combines her own participation in the sport with teaching at George Morris's Hunterdon Inc. in Pittstown, New Jersey.

Whereas many of the leading American riders teach for purely economic reasons, Anne has a dual purpose in that she also loves teaching, and the obvious pleasure she derives from this side of her equestrianism is self-evident when watching her help a pupil.

Far left: Anne and Starman in action at the Seoul Olympics, 1988, where they won a team silver medal and finished fourth in the individual competition.

Left: Anne and George Morris, in Korea for the Olympics in 1988, discuss the obstacles that lie ahead before the competition.

Above: "Here Suzanne Bond and I are working on a turning exercise – this is for both horse and rider. She will ride a figure 8, jumping a fence from the same direction but alternating between a left and right turn as she rides the figure 8, without stopping. Gradually one can tighten the turns and increase the angle of approach to the jump, depending on the abilities of the horse and rider."

Coaching in the United States is virtually a standard practice, with the less experienced Grand Prix riders, amateur and junior jumpers receiving comprehensive help in a way seldom seen in Europe. Even if riders do not regularly visit their trainers' bases, they are more than likely to be met at a show and taken right through the day, starting with the initial working-in period and finishing with a post-mortem after the competition.

In May 1989, at the Old Salem Show, which is held in an attractive tree-lined amphitheatre on Paul Greenwood's beautiful estate near Danville, Connecticut, Anne was not only competing but coaching Australian international Suzanne Bond, who had entered two horses in a combined junior amateur class.

At 8.00 a.m., in a far-flung exercise arena, the initial work began. Suzanne is circling in sitting trot. "Ride from your seat and use your legs more," counsels Anne. "Use your legs in rhythm with your seat. The moment your horse cuts in on the circle, push him out."

Suzanne progresses to a small circle, employing leg yielding. "You bend all your horses' necks too much; get him straighter with your leg," Anne continues. "Now change rein, left leg, yield out and passage; all the

time be aware where your horse's nose, shoulders and legs are. Look where you are going, just as you do when you are driving your car; look in the mirror.

"Halt. Good. Now move into posting trot. Don't let him pull you forward; he's getting sharper, so you have got to get a little softer. Bend him in a shorter, tighter circle right round; use your outside rein and leg. Now gradually enlarge the circle. Halt, canter from halt, and again. Sitting trot; sit down in the saddle with your legs a little more forward. That's okay, but the transition was abrupt. Lengthen your canter, keep your heels down, come into a tiny circle, do two, keep your length, and then enlarge the circle."

Anne puts up a jump of low crossed poles. "Come in on an angle, left to right, in trot," she directs. Suzanne jumps. "Get your body further forward, you're a little behind the motion. That's much better. Be sure to use your outside aids. Now I want you to take the jump at a more acute angle."

The jump is changed to a small oxer 2ft 6in (0.8m) high and 1ft 6in (0.5m) wide. The instruction is to jump straight. "Drop his mouth and let him come to it. Yes, good; loose, smooth and forward looking. Stop. This time use a left lead and left turn and outside aids.

Land, make a right and keep it short. I want to see you hunt at the jump, and, while keeping loose and smooth, really gallop to it."

Suzanne's groom takes her horse away, and rider and trainer set off to walk and analyse the course.

COURSE WALK

Fence 1 is a vertical with a short, left-hand turn to Fence 2, an oxer. Then it's right to Fence 3, a triple, with Fence 4, a vertical, coming quickly after. Fence 5 is the combination, an oxer to an oxer to a vertical, set slightly uphill. A sharp, right-hand turn follows to Fence 6, a vertical, and another sharp right-hand turn to Fence 7, an airy vertical. On to Fence 8, a dropped cross-pole oxer, then slightly to the left to Fence 9, which is almost a star. Left to Fence 10, a double of up-rights with the unsighting and distracting lake on the right, then slightly uphill to the final Fence 11, a vertical.

Above: "Here Suzanne is jumping the fence in the centre, slightly angled from right to left. Already she is looking ahead to where she wants to go next. Her right leg is on her horse's side, and her right rein is against the neck, helping to swing the shoulder around to the left."

Left: Anne is pleased with Suzanne's final practice jump on her grey thoroughbred Gandolf at Old Salem.

137

Above: Anne helps Suzanne by analysing the round she has just jumped at Old Salem.

Below right: Anne paces out the distance during a course walk at the Seoul Olympics.

Far right: Anne and Starman at the Royal Windsor Horse Show. The confidence and cooperation that is essential to a great partnership is etched on the faces of both horse and rider as they clear a jump in perfect harmony under the castle.

"Take the triple Fence 3 in the middle. Remember that good horses like yours don't have to jump mountains. Fence 4 is up the hill away from the entrance gate, so be sure your horses don't drift left.

"The combination comes up quickly, so think forward; it's not big but you need to ride more strongly. There is a nice one stride between the oxers, then take a steady two to the vertical. You don't jump until the twenties, so we'll have plenty of time to look and see how the course is riding. But here, drop his mouth and let him pick the stride.

"It's a nice seven strides on to Fence 6, then just follow the track on to Fences 7 and 8. Definitely take Fence 8 on the right-hand side or it will ride like a big oxer.

"Keep your momentum going round this left-hand curve to Fence 9. The lake is discon-

certing and could easily divert your horse's concentration and attention, so don't trust Gandolf on the approach to the double, Fence 10; stay behind him and really use your legs. As over the whole course, there is a lot for him to look at and you must be prepared for this, whether you are in the air or on the ground. Then it's six strides uphill to the final Fence 11.

"If you reach the jump-off, there is a lot to look at. If you take a tricky cut, you'll lose out. Come in fast to Fence 1. Overall, I'd prefer a slightly longer route and a fast gallop. There are plenty of alternatives. I think you should fly to the double, once you are on line, and then get a fast time up the following hill. Both your horses and you are well able to do this."

Anne goes on to explain, "When I teach, I try to think of a free horse jumping forward loose, not too regimented, but more forward and onward going. Right now, I'm trying to smooth Suzanne out a little; for my standard, she sits a little backwards. I want her to be slightly more foward-bound, rather than adopting the traditional Australian backward seat as she is now."

Anne and Suzanne settle down under a tree on the bank to watch how the first dozen competitors fare and finally define Suzanne's strategy. "Suzanne, the time is fine; I want your round to be controlled and simple, but don't get a time fault. The double of verticals by the lake is tight; go steady from the approach and there on to the last. Also get steady for the planks – Fence 4 – before the combination on that left-hand curve. Be sure to stay out."

Her final advice is, "The jumps are quite low. You can manage this course very easily, so keep it smooth; there is nothing very difficult, nothing you can't do." Suzanne intercedes, "I like an oxer for my first jump so that I can ride at it". She then leaves to remount and tune-up her grey thoroughbred, Gandolf.

Anne follows her to the nearest schooling ring and after watching a rival male rider execute a stuffy jump comments, "I didn't like that at all. You must do the opposite and keep going forward. Let him gallop away from the jump and then go forward. Don't forget that this is Gandolf's fourth day running, so he is bound to be a little tired. Think forward all the time. He tends to go a shade to both sides, but he's gradually getting straighter because of the way you are riding him. Above all, concentrate on going forward. The entrance to the double by the lake is very important because most of the horses are tiring there and could easily spook."

Suzanne gradually warms up Gandolf, progressing from walk and trot to canter, ending with several angled and then two straight, flowing jumps. She then spends two minutes watching the preceding competitor from the narrow gully alongside the ring before she is on her way.

ROUND ASSESSMENT

Suzanne arrives back up the bank and explains, "I took five strides not six because there have been very few clears and I was thinking of time and the lower placings." Anne sums up, "Overall, you did well. All the way round you had much more between your hands and your legs".

Suzanne moves off to prepare her second horse, and Anne continues, "Suzanne has some lovely horses. My biggest aim is to give her more confidence and to improve some basic points, such as keeping smooth and getting her position absolutely correct so that it doesn't interfere with her riding. It's a very simple, classical system; basically, we work to 12 feet [3.6m] a stride.

"With all my students, I stress that this is an extremely mental sport. The top winners are all very cool under pressure and stick to it whether they are at the Olympic Games or a little local show.

"The Ian Millars do it time and again. Our top riders, such as Rodney Jenkins and Joe Fargis, invariably stick to it and never allow themselves to get rattled.

"I enjoy teaching," concludes Anne. "I get a kick out of watching my riders improve and I believe that teaching improves my own riding, develops my subconscious and gives me the advantage of talking to other riders and teachers. Then, too, when your competitive career is over, you have another outlet. It's all so interesting, because each horse is totally different and you have to learn how to get the most out of it, and when teaching, how to match its qualities to those of its rider to the maximum advantage."

139

GREG BEST

Greg possesses great natural flair and enthusiasm. He has a good foundation from hunters and ponies, which includes equitation, and is a positive-thinking rider. He doesn't get bogged down with technicalities and if something goes wrong, he gets through somehow and presses on. He is a galloping rider like Frank Chapot, his mentor.

Horses work for him because of his consistent, free, forward approach. He believes in his horses, so they do more for him than perhaps they would for a more exact, technical rider. It's refreshing that he can ride through a problem where so many others cannot.

George Morris

At the age of 24, at the Seoul Olympics in 1988, Greg Best catapulted into the record books with Frank Chapot's Gem Twist by adding the individual silver medal to his team silver with a brave, bold, attacking and breathtaking jump-off round. It was an amazing performance by a rider of scant international experience who only two years previously had been riding at local shows near his Farmington, New Jersey, home.

The main Olympic arena was a far cry from his early days, when he was taught by his mother, a very successful pony trainer. Her sister, Mae, gave Greg a pony and, with the counsel of Colonel John Russell, who helped her with the basics, Greg's mother took her son through pony, junior hunter and equitation classes on ponies she was lent because they could not afford their own.

When Greg was 16 years old he went to Frank Chapot, his current mentor, who lives just half an hour's drive away, and started with novice jumpers. A graduate of the University of Pennsylvania, he is at present concentrating on show jumping but hopes that sometime in the future he will find a role combining his interest in the horse industry with his business degree. Right now, however, he is enjoying himself, finds everything fresh and exciting and feels he still has a lot to learn about horses and the horse world.

Greg credits Frank with having given him a great depth of knowledge of horses in general: "He has an all-encompassing knowledge and a broad way of thinking. He doesn't dictate or brainwash; he encourages independent thinking."

Greg says that Frank's biggest problem was getting him to sit properly. "It was my weakest point and it still is. I spent hours and hours, day after day, week after week on the

Far left: Greg and Gem Twist on their way to the individual silver medal on the final day at Seoul, 1988. Greg comments that Gem Twist "has such a big jump he doesn't have to fold his legs to his chin to clear the jumps all that often".

Left: Greg and Gem Twist at home. The grey benefits from the fact that he is not over-jumped, but prepared very carefully for specific major targets.

141

lunge with no stirrups. I'd end up too tired to stand and in the end, I learnt how to sit because I couldn't stand any more."

Riding a great many horses, including bad ones that no one else has wanted to ride, has made him an aggressive rider in the same mould as Frank Chapot. "My motto, my philosophy, is to be very aggressive and to attack the course."

Frank has bred many horses from his ebullient stallion Good Twist and his offspring, and Greg thinks that Frank's handling and

training of them has influenced his teaching. Greg himself has followed the same pattern, riding many of Good Twist's sons and daughters in his formative years, such as Easter Twist and Snappy Twist.

SELECTION

With a flow of Frank's largely home-bred horses at his disposal, Greg has selected only three or four horses to date. One of these is his current number two string, Red Rose Farm's Holsteiner Santos, a good Grand Prix horse who makes an excellent back-up and alternative to Gem Twist, who inevitably overshadows him.

Greg had seen Santos ridden by Frank's elder daughter, Wendy, when she had him for a year in junior jumpers, and thought that he was very honest. "For me it's most important that the horse jumps at all times; when I make a mistake, he must keep going. I didn't know how much ability he had. Frank always advises me not to count on making a horse better but to hope to keep him at the level he's at."

Clearly Greg succeeded in raising Santos's level because there were 70 horses in the final Grand Prix at Tampa in 1987 and Gem Twist was first and Santos second. Two years

Right: Greg (left), Leslie Burr Lenehan (centre) and Frank Chapot (right) in conversation during a course walk at the Volvo World Cup final at Tampa, Florida, 1989.

Below: Frank Chapot rides Gem Twist away from the stables, which are in the attractive Dutch-style converted barn. Following Frank are his two daughters, Laura and Wendy, both of whom feature regularly in the ribbons.

later, Greg rated the course to be one of the biggest he had ever jumped.

Temperament is paramount to Greg, who likes a horse with a lot of heart and which tries hard. "An ounce of heart is worth a pound of ability." His ideal horse is not only able to jump a big jump but has the right attitude and the desire to perform.

"A lot of horses have more ability than Gem Twist but Gem always tries his very hardest. That's what makes him a great horse; he wants to be one and wants to clear the jumps. When Frank and I brought along Gem Twist, we were never in a rush because as I had never been to international level, I couldn't be hurried. This was a good step for both of us because we were both learning. Gem had a full year in low school, then intermediate, and in the fourth year, in February 1987, began Grand Prix in Florida. Frank was responsible for most of Gem's low school year."

Carefulness is very important to Greg. "Ian Millar's Big Ben is physically careful and Gem Twist is very careful. Then there are horses who continually defy the laws and are not the prettiest to watch, perhaps with bad conformation; they are freaks."

With his attacking, aggressive approach, speed classes are one of Greg's strengths. "I love them; the thrill of speed is so exciting,

Above and left: Two studies in exuberance – in the loose school (above) and in the well-railed paddock (left). There is a floating population of about 50 horses at Frank's Neshanic Station, New Jersey, stables.

143

going in and galloping round the course. My riding style is a gallop; I just go in and pick a stride and keep going wider round the course than the others and take a longer route than they do with longer curves, but it's the consistent pace I maintain that gets me there faster. The pressure in my individual silver-medal-winning round at Seoul was overwhelming. I still have far too little international experience."

TRAINING AND COMPETITION

Training Gem Twist pivots on getting the grey gelding as fit and healthy as possible, because "In the ring he takes care of himself. He is incredibly careful, that's his biggest asset; he does not want to hit jumps – and he is capable of jumping anything that anyone can build."

Problems are non-existent when Gem is 100 per cent fit and, say those who know him, he loves to please and senses a big occasion

Above: Greg and Gem Twist in the practice field at Neshanic Station. They are preparing to jump a line of distance-related fences.

Right: Gem Twist already has his attention fixed on the next fence as he arches his neck in a bascule during the Seoul Olympics, 1988.

like the Games or A.G.A. Championships. "It's like night and day; he recognizes the difference between a big class and a little class."

At home Gem is seldom schooled over any jumps of more than medium height: he has so much innate ability that it is not necessary.

One unusual difficulty that Gem has is a tendency to overreach and pull off his off-fore front shoe. This has happened in Grand Prix in both initial rounds and in jump-offs. In the 1989 Tampa Invitational, which he won in conclusive fashion, this occurred just before the jump-off, when his reappearance was delayed while the shoe was replaced.

No show jumper is immune to off days but Greg is more resilient than many of his rivals because "By the law of averages, a better horse has fewer bad days, and I find Gem Twist so exciting because he can win anywhere in the world. He can win with ease at both indoor and outdoor jumping.

"When things go wrong in the ring," explains Greg, "I turn into an aggressive rider concerned to get round in one piece. In the second round of the individual in Seoul, Gem was bucking. I thought he was tired; the adrenalin was flowing, and when I jumped the first fence rather badly, I realized that I had to forget I was at the Olympics and get round well." Conversely, Frank Chapot thinks that Gem was not tired but bucking because, under stress, Greg was not sitting in the right place in the saddle.

There is no doubt that everyone experiences pressure riding for the first time at the Olympics, and Greg, who reached the top so suddenly, is no exception.

The 1987 Pan-American Games in Indianapolis, at which Greg and Gem were members of the U.S. silver-medal-winning team, was his first serious test of competing under intense pressure. At that time, Greg had competed in only nine or ten Grand Prix, and "It was the first time I'd ridden with a flag under my saddle. But, in a way, by the time I'd reached the Games, I'd had more experience than the record books show because my success, when it came, came so fast, with a lot of media attention to which I was unaccustomed and had to get used."

The 1990 World Championships at Stockholm provided Greg and Gem Twist's first major target in the new decade. The U.S. team, racked by a continuing selection dispute, lost their title, finishing fourth behind France, West Germany and Britain. Then, after the last individual competition, Greg found himself heading the field prior to the four-rider change-horse contest for the individual medals: exactly the same position Pierre Durand had been in at this stage in the 1986 World Championships in Aachen. Pierre had finished fourth, and Greg was to do the same, finishing behind France's Eric Navet (gold) and Hubert Bourdy (bronze), with John Whitaker receiving the silver for Britain.

Greg, who surely did not deserve to travel home from Stockholm empty-handed, incurred faults on all four horses – including two on Milton, who he had been looking forward to riding. Greg blamed himself for the latter errors, saying he had not ridden the grey with sufficient aggression. He still managed to be cheerful in defeat: "It's like having a date with the most beautiful woman in the world – you trip over your feet a few times".

Left: Smiles on the victory rostrum after the Olympic individual show-jumping contest in Seoul in 1988. From left to right are Greg (silver), Pierre Durand (France, gold) and Karsten Huck (Germany, bronze).

FRANK CHAPOT

The breeding of Gem Twist has given Frank Chapot an enduring personal interest and involvement in the sport which has long been, and is still, his life – an opportunity for which any former Olympic rider would give his eye teeth.

There has been no more illustrious, determined or enduring rider. A six-times Olympian, having competed at Stockholm in 1956, Rome in 1960, Tokyo in 1964, Mexico in 1968, Munich in 1972 and Montreal in 1976, he was a member of the United States' silver-medal-winning teams at Rome and Munich, on Trail Guide and White Lightning respectively.

Frank has made a phenomenal 98 Nations' Cup appearances, which is a record, 45 of them winning ones. He was fourth in the Mexico Olympics on San Lucas and fifth in the Montreal Olympics on Viscount. In 1974,

at Hickstead, he was equal third in the World Championships and won the King George V Gold Cup at the Royal International Horse Show with Mainspring in 1974.

Now he combines breaking and training show jumpers, taking clinics and judging with acting as *chef d'équipe* at the major shows. He has filled this role at every World Cup Final from the inaugural year at Gothenburg in 1979 onwards. Currently he is concerned about the stressing of horses now that there is an established winter season and barely any rest. He thinks that there should not be additional world competitions in years when there are Olympic Games and World Championships, in order to reduce pressure on the top horses.

Citing Ian Millar's 1988 and 1989 World Cup winner Big Ben as an example, Frank thinks that the effort necessary at the former event contributed to Big Ben's failure to finish

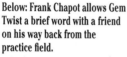

Below: Frank Chapot allows Gem Twist a brief word with a friend on his way back from the practice field.

higher in the Seoul Olympics, which were held approximately halfway between the two World Cup Finals. He considers Millar to have done a wonderful job getting Ben so fresh to win the World Cup at Tampa in 1989. Like many riders, he was concerned about the proximity of the World Cup Final in Dortmund, Germany, in April 1990 to the World Championships in Stockholm, Sweden, the following July–August.

Frank is also a respected international course designer and this, combined with his experience of the world of show jumping, has played an invaluable and integral part in the development of Gem Twist and Greg Best into one of the world's outstanding show-jumping combinations.

Frank lives at Neshanic Station, New Jersey, with his wife, the former international Mary Mairs, and their two daughters – Wendy, who is 21, and Laura, who is two years younger. The whole family are horse orientated; they have a floating population of about 50 horses, and most weeks the girls compete at shows.

The main stables, 28 in number, are in a tall, converted Dutch-style cow barn. There is a small, separate three-stall area for quarantining and a big indoor school with a viewing room. The house and buildings are set in 50 rolling green acres.

Regarding Greg, Frank feels sure that he will improve further as he gets more competition, particularly overseas. He hopes that Greg will receive offers to ride top-class horses besides Santos and Gem. "Miles on the clock are what he needs, but good horses are so few and far between that, sadly, the world doesn't beat on the door with offers."

Greg's hunter seat suits his and Frank's method of riding. The way that American hunter-class juniors are penalized early on if they flop their arms or stick out their legs pays dividends, so that composed, stylish riders are the rule rather than the exception.

When Frank and Greg work Gem, they are mindful that he has a very good eye of his own. Their approach is not to worry too much about strides and to let Gem's eyes work. This has proved successful, working far better than if Greg were all hands and messing about too much over distances. Such an approach is only viable if a rider and

Above: Frank and his wife Mary – a former international – give daughters Laura and Wendy some special tips at home.

Left: Balance, control and pace are encapsulated in this shot of Greg and Gem Twist executing a time-saving turn at Seoul in 1988.

147

Above: Frank Chapot sets up a practice fence for Greg and Gem Twist to jump (see sequence below). The fence is a remarkable 7ft 6in (2.3m) wide.

Below: This six-shot sequence of Greg and Gem jumping the fence constructed by Frank (see above) illustrates the exceptional class of the combination. The jump is executed with an ease that suggests that they are in no way extended to their maximum by Frank's fence.

his horse's eyes are in perfect synchronization, which is the case almost all the time with this combination; whereas, on a horse that lacks scope, this tactic could court trouble.

Frank says that "Greg is game, bold, hungry, has confidence and wants to win. He felt he would go well – could beat everyone – in the 1989 World Cup Final, but, ominously, he was drawn late in the first round, and when he approached Fence 3 the footing had gone, and with it his chance of victory."

Frank and Greg are fortunate that Gem has a good owner in Michael Golden, who supports the horse and gives Greg a percentage of the winnings. Mr Golden bought Gem to handle himself but found him too difficult, hence his return to Frank's tutelage.

Frank taught and encouraged Gem to have an eye of his own, which he considers to be of paramount importance. He also progressed to changes of lead in the grey's flatwork and took him to his early shows.

Then, however, Gem's jumping began to hurt Frank's back because the grey picks up his hindquarters so high. "By this time," recalls Frank, "Greg was a natural, tailor-made to take over the ride because he had grown up in his late teens riding a bunch of horses by Good Twist". However, Frank still does some of Gem's flatwork himself.

Because of the many horses Frank has bred over the years, he has tended to choose from these rather than going out and buying with any frequency. Ideally, Frank likes a horse to have scope and to be careful, because for him that is what training jumpers is all about. "I like enough chicken so that when a horse comes down to a jump it will try not to touch it, but, conversely, if a horse is too brave, he may not care enough and not worry if he hits a jump."

Soundness is another criterion, and his horses must have no real conformation defects.

Training

Frank and Greg work Gem Twist on gymnastic lines. Along the narrow lane below the house there is a jumping area in a field dappled with wild flowers. Frank sets a vertical, then, a normal steady three strides on, an oxer 3ft 6in (1.1m) high by 7ft 6in (2.3m) wide. "There is no need to drive, Greg," Frank advises, "try to sit still and let the horse figure this out for himself; don't ride at it. Sit quietly and let Gem's eye do the work."

Left: Frank (left) with Greg and Gem Twist, standing under the trees that give West Palm Beach its name, discuss their priorities for the ensuing early morning school. Greg and Gem are now sponsored by Moët et Chandon.

He switches the subject as he questions, "Who would send a horse from the States to Korea not wrapped in cotton wool?", and answers his own question with a degree of pride: "Me. Gem is never shipped in bandages because he doesn't like them. The only bandages he ever wears are occasional rest bandages in front, never behind because he particularly dislikes those. He is easy to care for, nice in his stall, and to groom, and doesn't go crazy when turned out."

Pressure

Frank describes the conditions at the 1987 Pan-American Games in Indianapolis: "There was a lot of pressure because the U.S. team was supposed to win – we were heavy favourites. Greg had won the final trial and was meant to be a star, so he felt immense pressure at his first major international. To make matters worse, the footing was lousy. It was very disconcerting for Greg, because in some parts of the arena the sand was six inches [15cm] deep and in others only two [5cm]. Greg was understandably very nervous. Then when he was in a position to win after the first day, it put on more pressure."

At the Seoul Olympic Games, Greg was in with a chance of a medal win. The jump-off course to decide the destiny of the silver and bronze medals was not "too high or wide, and there were some of the long curves which I knew would suit Greg and Gem. If you can

Right: Greg and Gem Twist clear an oxer at the Seoul Olympics, 1988. Greg comments that "you can see where he could get into trouble because he can get too high, so we just don't make the width".

Below: It is seldom that Greg (left) and Frank look so solemn. Frank has been Greg's mentor since the latter first attended Frank's stables when he was 16.

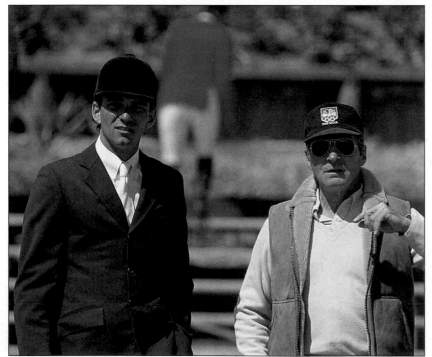

only ride one way, some course builder will get you in the end. Greg and I work together on the premise that if you have a chest full of tools and you add a new tool, you improve the other tools, and the wider the range of tools, the better the carpenter. You have to be able to leave out or add strides and, by 1988, Greg was well able to do this.

"Continuing analysis is crucial. At the 1989 World Cup Final in Tampa, the course included a combination of a vertical with one stride to another vertical and, 32ft [9.7m] on, a very wide oxer, where Gem had the back rail down because Greg drove too much."

The Breeding of Gem Twist

Gem Twist's breeding is of especial interest because, at the beginning of the nineties, he rates as one of the world's top horses, of the same rare echelon as Big Ben, Jappeloup, Milton and Walzerkönig.

Frank bought his sire, Good Twist, from Ben O'Meara as a 3-year-old for a customer –

but kept him. He proved to be one of the best horses that Frank has ever had, jumped internationally until he was 17 years old, and scored one of his most spectacular victories when he won the New York Grand Prix in 1972. A grey thoroughbred, Good Twist stood only 15.1 hands high.

He proved to be a real foundation sire of the Bon Nuit line, the members of which, to name but a few of those who made themselves international reputations, include Miss Budweiser, who carried Arthur McCashin to a team bronze medal at the Helsinki Olympics, Hollandia, on who Bill Steinkraus also won a team bronze medal at the same Olympics, Riviera Wonder, who won the International German Championship in 1959 with Bill Steinkraus, and Night Owl, on whom Bill Steinkraus put up the best performance in the U.S. team that was placed fifth at the Stockholm Olympics in 1956. In an era when titles were won or lost through rubs, this equestrian family were known for being very clean jumpers – the equivalent of 'careful' at the beginning of the nineties.

At the time he had Good Twist, Frank was trying to build a little herd of thoroughbred mares to provide horses for Mary, himself and his daughters to have some fun with, and also some to educate and sell on.

The pre-eminent qualities that Good Twist passed on were carefulness and a desire to win. Typical of his offspring, Gem is not a horse who fights or resists when it is necessary to go fast. This makes all the difference between winning and losing.

Gem Twist's dam is the thoroughbred Coldly Noble, a racehorse given to Frank by the grandmother of Joy Carrier of Grand National fame. In 1989, she had a foal of Good News, a son of Good Twist.

Whereas the winning U.S. teams of the seventies were renowned for their wonderfully schooled thoroughbreds, largely bought off the tracks, during the eighties the scene changed. Today, the supply of racehorses has diminished, because there are now many more racetracks in the United States; and the lower-grade tracks soak up many of the horses found wanting at the major ones. This is the category of horse that formerly came into show jumping at this stage in their careers. "There is often so much medication used at the cheaper tracks that there is little left of the horses by the time they have finished racing."

Below: Frank at home in New Jersey with some stock that has been bred on similar lines to Gem Twist.

MICHAEL MATZ

I did not train Michael, but he and I have a joint interest in the help we have both been fortunate enough to enjoy from Bert de Nemethy. Michael is one of my favourite show jumpers, a master horseman and a beautiful rider and trainer – a trainer whose priority is always to consider his horse and who never overjumps.

He is a great hunter man. Vince Dugan and Bernie Traurig were his early trainers. He has an innate smoothness, rides in a hunter-seat style and is also an equitation rider, which is a great combination. Bert de Nemethy helped with his dressage and gymnastic work. Bert made him an international star.

Michael couples power and strength with a subtleness and smoothness; he is one of the world's greatest.

George Morris

No one in Michael's family has any equestrian association or interest. When he was 15 years old at high school, he had a job cutting lawns for a friend's father whose wife had a horse. She was on the point of giving up riding and asked Michael to ride her horse. Michael remembers, "I had a go because I thought I would lose the job if I did not and I needed the money. Then I went to several local shows, saw the kids jumping and knew that I could do better. I built myself one jump of telegraph poles – they were so heavy that I could not roll them or lift them higher."

Michael was soon competing at small shows, completely motivated and on his way. As soon as he was 17 years old and out of high school, he was lucky to be introduced to a top-class international rider, when he went and worked for six months for one of the leading show jumpers in the United States, Bernie Traurig.

He then took a job near home, clipping, braiding, mucking out and exercising, "to make some dollars". His parents lent him $3,000 to buy a horse and found him a job in Florida, where he could take the horse. He worked for Vince Dugan, who had a sales barn, and gained valuable experience riding "tons and tons of horses all of different types. I jumped all the time and gradually began to go better as I learnt to control the various horses I rode."

Michael then met Jerry Baker, who "polished me up. I trained horses for him and he spent lots of time working with me on the flat." Once Michael had learnt the correct mechanics, he found that everything became easier. "One thing that helped me then and helps me now is that I have the ability to be aware of what is going on around me. I notice

Far left: Liran is giving all he has got to a determined Michael Matz in a 1989 Grand Prix jump-off at West Palm Beach.

Left: Michael and Chef about to go into the ring at the World Championships in Aachen in 1986. Michael's jaw is set as he thinks about the forthcoming challenge in the continent's premier permanent arena. Chef has a wonderful readiness, enthusiasm and intelligence written on his face.

Above: Michael riding out at home in Collegeville, Pennsylvania. His eye for detail has made his enterprise one of the world's most immaculate and best-maintained.

Below: Bonne Retour has many of the qualities Michael considers all-important. Note here, for example, the chestnut's sloping shoulder, straight hind leg and short coupling.

detail very fast, every detail about the barn, a horse, a flat tyre, what someone is or is not doing. Whatever else, I want my barns to be neat, and my first concern is my horses' well-being. Maybe I'm too picky, but whatever I'm doing I keep my standards very high."

Jerry Baker and Bert de Nemethy, who Michael met when he was selected to train and ride for the U.S.E.T. at Gladstone, were those who helped Michael develop most of his flatwork. "Bert was responsible for teaching me my dressage, cavaletti and gymnastic work." All Bert's riders either had or developed style, and he was a profound influence on Michael at this time. When Bert trained the U.S.E.T., everything was superbly organized, and when Michael went to ride Mr Howard Ward's horses for Jerry Baker, it was the same. "They ran a tight ship, which is the way it should be, and this moulded and directed me enormously in my formative years. When I look back, I realize that I have been very fortunate in the people by whom I have been surrounded all the time."

It was Jerry Baker who helped Michael develop both basic and fundamental horse sense, something which was not innate. From him he also learnt to use the horse's back to full advantage. At the time, Mr Baker only had eight horses, which meant that Michael had plenty of time to concentrate on each one and make them go well.

SELECTION

Michael looks for horses all the time. When he went to pick a yearling for a racing project, he looked at 3,000 before he made a choice. He likes a classic type, and while he prefers a horse 16.2 hands high, much can depend on how the horse carries itself.

His conformation priorities are a sloping shoulder, a short rump, a straight hind leg and an equal triangle from hip to gaskin to rump. Whether he is looking for show jumping or racing, Michael will not entertain a

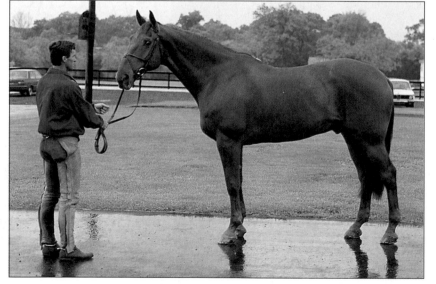

horse that is back at the knee, much preferring one that is over.

He finds assessing temperament difficult. "It's like looking into someone's face to see their personality; it is just as hard as it is with people, and you do not have the advantage of being able to talk to them. If you are able to have the horse in your stable for a week, you will probably get to know his personality, but if you do not, it is unlikely.

"There is a first-class racing example. Look at Mr Arthur B. Hancock III's Sunday Silence, who narrowly failed to win the 1989 triple crown after triumphing in the Kentucky Derby and the Preakness Stakes. Nobody wanted to train him at first because he is unfashionably bred by Halo out of the Understanding mare Wishing Well. But, just as I believe that good show jumpers eventually find their way into the better riders' stables, so this outstanding horse was eventually trained by Californian trainer Charlie Whittingham, who is at the top of the tree." In November, 1989, Sunday Silence won the most valuable international thoroughbred race in the world – the Breeders' Cup Classic, at Gulf Stream Park, Hallandale, north of Miami, Florida, which is worth $1.1 million to the winner.

Michael searches for a horse that moves easily across the ground because he has found over the years that horses who do not move well almost always have problems.

Jet Run, who he rates as his best show jumper ever, was a big powerful horse, very strong with abundant stamina. Yet whilst "a delight to ride in competition, [Jet Run] was hard to contain on the flat at home, partly because his attention span was very short".

Michael also puts much more stress on carefulness than when he first competed internationally, his change of attitude dating from the 1976 Montreal Olympics, "where so many good horses and riders were on the floor". The reason for this was a change in course designing entailing the use of much lighter equipment, a development which has gradually gained momentum since then until a situation has developed whereby the emphasis is now on carefulness with fewer big fences.

Unlike many other show jumpers, he is quite prepared to buy really young horses

and take his time with them. He considers himself privileged to have understanding and trusting owners who are 100 per cent behind him in this and not pushing for results, "rather than back-seat drivers".

Generalizing, Michael's favourite horses for show jumping are thoroughbreds. This is because he finds they have more blood and have that little bit more fight in them. "I am also influenced by the fact that they are a little finer and more beautiful, easier on the eye. I don't think you will ever see me on a pinto or an appaloosa unless it's a stunner."

The exceptional Jet Run was not selected but came to him because a Mexican friend, Fernando Senderos, who had won the individual gold medal on him at the 1975 Pan-American Games at Mexico City with some training help from Michael, had to turn his

Below: Each spring, the Florida Sunshine Circuit offers excellent classes for horses of all degrees of experience. Here Michael is schooling an attentive grey in the collecting ring at the West Palm Beach arena.

attention to running the family's business empire and no longer had available the very considerable amount of time necessary for competitive show jumping.

Jet Run had been based with Michael for much of the time Fernando rode him, and as his owner did not want to see his great horse wasted, he offered him to Michael. Jerry Baker and Michael asked Mr Dixon – the man who had paid a king's ransom for the famed Philadelphia 56ers – if he would buy him, and Mr Dixon replied, "No matter if the price is steep, if the horse is as good as you say he is, I'd better have him."

Michael had to persist with Jet Run, who was as quick as lightning, even over small fences. The first time he sat on the horse, Michael's nose was broken when Jet Run jumped and threw his head back when surprised by a trash truck dumping rubbish. The horse needed an infinite amount of work, far more than most show jumpers. He had

Above: Michael on Jet Run at Hickstead in 1982. Jet Run, Michael recalls, was one of show jumping's all-time greats: "He knew what to do and had his own way of doing it".

Right: Ghostbuster, the Hanoverian that Michael has been bringing on for Mexican Fernando Senderos, at West Palm Beach in 1989.

terrific stamina – only five minutes after completing a course he was ready to go again.

When Michael took over the ride, Jet Run was already nine years old, a senior horse who had been shown for five years, graduating to big classes and the Olympic Games with Fernando. Remarkably, he could not execute flying changes, and for much of the time proceeded at a cross canter; but as he had so much natural ability, at that stage of his career this did not matter. "He knew what to do and had his own way of doing it, which was not the best way. I was always riding him off the seat of my pants; he did not have sufficient discipline for me to get the very best from him."

Few show jumpers are fortunate to have the ride on a great horse, a Big Ben, Gem Twist or Milton, for the duration of their entire careers. Michael had Jet Run from 1977, after the Montreal Olympics, until 1985, when he was retired, aged 17, to Mr Dixon's farm. There he lives in luxury with another of Michael's former multi-winning mounts, Grande. In 1979, Michael, like Fernando, won the Pan-American Games individual gold medal on Jet Run, the event this time being held in Puerto Rico.

Although Jet Run proved to be insufficiently disciplined for Michael's style of riding, he had gone very well for Fernando, a very light and sympathetic rider to whom horses respond. Michael soon discovered that although Jet Run was supple in a way, he had to give him much more flatwork than usual to instil discipline in order to ride him as well as he wished.

Jet Run's biggest asset was perhaps not his enormous scope but the fact that he was, above all, a winner. Even great riders and great horses need time to form an effective partnership. The first time Michael rode Jet Run in public was at Mason Phelps' famous Derby. "Jet Run was nervous when a horse came towards him, or at him. This happened in the schooling area just as I had directed him towards a jump; then, his attention diverted, he ran out. Jerry Baker called out to me, 'Michael, whatever are you doing? This is Jet Run.'"

However, once he was through the starting gates and on his own in the main arena, he was all business in what proved an exceptionally long career, because he was a very sound horse. Michael tried for the 1984 Olympics with him, "but it was not to be. Now I realize that 12 years top-level jumping is enough for any horse."

TRAINING

Michael tries to keep all his training work as simple as possible and thinks that riders can all too easily make it far more difficult than it need be.

In the summer of 1989, Fernando Senderos had nine horses in training, some in Europe and some with Michael in preparation for his return to the sport, with the aim of winning a place in the Mexican team for the 1992 Olympic Games. The strong, eight-year-old Hanoverian Ghostbuster is one of those Michael has been schooling for Fernando. His basic training routine is a sequence of gymnastic exercises, beginning with the walk and halts

Above left: Karen Golding (right), Michael's stable manager, discusses a tight day's schedule with her boss.

Left: Michael training a youngster at home. Note the use of a small spread until the horse has completely mastered the jump.

Above: Using trotting poles at home to control the horse's pace and get the stride right.

people working for him, fronted by his long-time barn manager, Karen Golding, and good owners. And, as the New Bolton Veterinary Center is just down the road, expert help is at hand when any unexpected problems arise. He is well aware of the odds against him but, as a firm believer in his oft-expressed theory that good horses come to good riders, he is optimistic that two or three of the youngsters might develop into international material.

Secondly, he has a relatively new and fast-growing interest in flat racing. This directly benefits his show jumping, because he has become increasingly aware of the value of 100 per cent fitness in show jumping, not only to enhance performance but to keep horses in competition for longer. "I figure that if my horses are fitter, they are fresher and the risk of injury is cut down."

Michael says that his horses are fitter than many others, perhaps the fittest on the American circuit. To attain this high level of fitness he sticks to a basic weekly schedule:

Monday The horses have a rest day in their boxes with only hay and water and no grain.

Tuesday The horses are worked on the flat and only jumped if there is a special need to do so.

Wednesday The young horses are schooled as necessary, perhaps worked on the flat or taken round the racehorse gallop at a slow canter, a steady canter or, occasionally, at a gallop.

Thursday and Friday Largely flatwork. Some jumping for horses competing on Saturday as required.

Saturday Competition.

Sunday Horses are turned out; bran mash in the evening.

Just as Michael applies some of the principles relating to the fitness of the racehorses in his care to his show jumpers, he does the reverse schooling to improve his racehorses. "We've all watched jockeys grab horses' mouths in races. I've tried to break my racehorses well and put on a little mouth. Then, if the jockey sees a gap in a race, he might manage to manoeuvre through with his better than average steering, which he might not be able to do otherwise."

Although Michael trains riders and is more than proud of his currently successful pupil Dina Santangelo, who has an extremely

and progressing to a sitting trot, medium trot and passage at the walk. Then there is cantering over five jumps, three low oxers and two verticals, with preceding poles on the ground in the centre of the large gallop-encircled area to help keep the horse alert as he faces frequent changes of lead. The stables at Collegeville, Pennsylvania, are surrounded by woods with intersecting trails, and Michael hacks his horses down them several times a week for relaxation and a refreshing change of scene.

Michael's many top-level achievements include winning the World Cup in 1981 on Jet Run and being a member of the U.S. gold-medal-winning team with Chef at the 1986 World Championships. He has been at the top for a long and honourable 19 seasons. He is now 40 years old, and at a stage in his career when many riders find it difficult to keep motivated and retain a sharp, competitive edge and enthusiasm. "When I feel I can't do justice to my horses, I shall stop show jumping", says Michael; but for two reasons, he has not yet experienced this problem.

First of all, he loves the sport. One of his barns contains 15 horses from four to eight years old, all of the right type, that he rates as very promising. Additionally, he has the right useful Grand Prix record with Manassas County, he prefers on the whole to work with horses rather than people. "I enjoy the building of a combination of horse and rider and find that one frustration of racing is having to throw up a little jockey who is just riding for the money when I have done so much schooling and background work."

Michael has five racehorses in his care, and Tukwila, in whom he has a 20 per cent share, has provided an encouraging start. He bought this chestnut, by Coastal, at Keeneland Sales as a yearling, broke him, and saw him go on to win two of his first four races.

"Sometimes I feel burnt out or fed up with show jumping – everyone does. And if someone not so good wins, it bugs me. Then I may go for a refreshing change of scene to a two-year-old sale." The mixture of the two equestrian sports suits Michael; each revitalizes his interest in the other. He is adamant, too, that "When I can't do justice to my show jumpers, I shall stop competing".

Meanwhile, he finds it enjoyable to look for young horses and bring them on. "I have to roll over – it only makes sense – and when Chef was sold to Joe Fargis, I bought two talented youngsters instead. I am really enjoying bringing them on."

ATTENTION TO DETAIL

Attention to even the most minute detail is Michael's hallmark and one of the keys to his success. His is probably the most immaculately maintained show-jumping yard in the United States. There isn't a weed or piece of straw in sight, the saddlery is soft and supple, and the horses are superbly cared for. Everything runs in the well-oiled manner which indicates that, behind the scenes, there is an all-knowing boss with a tight, but unobtrusive, discipline.

Bonne Retour, currently Michael's top international horse, is Argentinian-bred and was bought in Brazil. He is now owned by Mrs Helen Groves and her daughter D.D. Alexander. Attention to detail is evident in the unusual way in which this chestnut is shod. His front shoes have an unusual three clips, one centre front and one each side. This is to stop the shoes closing in at the heel end and to get, and keep, the bones in the hoof in the

correct line. Bonne Retour needs a high heel to ensure this happens, and the toe of the hoof has to be cut short.

Australian George Senna's Schnapps, who was based with Michael in 1989, has the same three-clenched shoe, but for a different reason. When he arrived he had insufficient hoof, and the three clips helped to hold on his shoes. Even so, his shoes are made with specially drilled holes to accommodate and grip the small nails that have to be used.

Michael had an eventful year in 1989, not all for the right reasons. He was in an air crash yet, a week later, won the Southampton Grand Prix. Shortly afterwards, he broke an ankle and was out of action for four months.

Left: Michael and Chef soaring over a huge spread at the World Championships, Aachen, 1986 – and helping the U.S. team to the gold medals. Michael and Chef also finished fifth individually.

Below: Michael, whose style embraces both subtlety and strength, keeps his head while jumping the Mercedes fence on Chef at Aachen in 1986.